Gabriele Rabkin

Far away from Home

Tibetan Refugee Children Write and Paint their Stories

Paljor Publications Pvt. Ltd.

New Delhi

This book is dedicated to
His Holiness the 14th Dalai Lama
on the occasion of his
seventieth birthday in the year 2005

THE DALAI LAMA

FOREWORD

It is now more than forty-five years since I and many of my compatriots left our homeland, Tibet, and embarked on a new life as refugees living in exile. To begin with we mostly lived near to one another in India and Nepal, but in the course of time the Tibetan refugee community has spread far and wide. There are now Tibetan communities in many parts of the world, and, as a result, there are many children who have grown up in quite different environments, but who share a common bond that they are Tibetan. When I visit these dispersed communities here and there, I find it very encouraging to see how determined our people are to maintain their Tibetan identity and how strong is the yearning, even among those who have not yet been there, to return to Tibet.

In this book, Dr. Gabriele Rabkin has collected stories and paintings done by Tibetan children of the Tibetan diaspora that depict vividly many of their concerns, hopes and aspirations. I feel optimistic that despite acquiring languages, customs and ambitions that may diverge from Tibetan tradition, most of the children who have expressed themselves here are motivated by the traditional Tibetan values of compassion and concern for others that are a source of hope and success. These stories and pictures will provide readers with a realistic view of life and opportunity many of these children have embraced in exile.

August 11, 2004

1)

[Valery Bugrov, "Heaven and Earth", 1991

6

During the Audience in Leh/Ladakh (27.5.1999)

Just as you are able to see
The multispheric types of forms in this mirror
Similarly in the mirror of the mind
We get different types of reflections [in the thought]
So if one were gently intelligent enough
To watch the mirror's thoughts
That come and go into the mind
That would be just amazing…

Spiritual Poem written by His Holiness, the 14th Dalai Lama[2]

[2] Written by His Holiness during my private
audience in Leh, Ladakh, 27.5.1999

8

Nechung Oracle

9

The world flower
Ven. Thupten Ngodub (Dharamsala)

Painted by Ven. Thupten Ngodub exclusively for
the project in March 2001

CONTENTS

1. INTRODUCTION

Being "far away from home" is a fate that Tibetan refugee children share with many other refugee children in other parts of the world. In this book Tibetan children in exile write and paint about their lives. Their creative work helps us to understand what is special about their fate and how they live in exile.

At the same time this book represents my very personal attitude towards Tibetan children. Over a period of five years I gathered wide experience of working with these children in different places including India, Nepal and Switzerland. This led to strong personal contacts, working relationships and friendships, which involved a deep personal sharing of their fates and contributed at the same time to my own development. The focus of my work is on the Tibetan Children's Village in Dharamsala, where for four years I accompanied a group of children, meeting and working with them every year.

The collection of paintings and stories in this volume was assembled through conversations with the children (the communication was carried out in English). Moreover, in Dharamsala it was possible to engage in a deep exchange of ideas with the local Tibetan experts in education.

A particularly important experience was the opportunity to present numerous pictures and stories to His Holiness the 14th Dalai Lama in person. His deep empathy with the thoughts and feelings of each child and his heartfelt sympathy with the idea of this project were of great significance to me. Inspired by the abundance of creative thoughts of the children, His Holiness the Dalai Lama spontaneously wrote a poem himself in the end of our meeting! The content of this poem touches miraculously upon the underlying aim of this book, which attempts carefully and sensitively to get closer to the inner world and thoughts of the Tibetan children who expressed themselves often symbolically in paintings and writings in so many diverse ways.

After an introduction into the present-day situation of the Tibetan refugees and the Tibetan mode of education in exile, a short description of the methodological approach is given. It is followed by a presentation of individual encounters and the creative work with the children. Then the emphasis is placed on the works of the children, which are arranged into various categories. In some works they express their personal feelings (love, homesickness, jealousy, etc.); in others they present their thoughts in the form of fairy-tales and dreams. The subjects of religion and love of nature play an important role, as do various aspects of social life, which sometimes also touch upon political issues. The poems at the end are mostly chosen from works by older pupils. The texts inspired by one particular picture are of special value, as it was drawn specially for this project with great empathy and interest by Ven. Thupten Ngodub, Medium of the State Oracle of His Holiness, the Dalai Lama ("Nechung Oracle").

12

[3] See page 1

2. TIBETAN CHILDREN IN EXILE

After the annexation of Tibet by China (1951) and the escape of the 14th Dalai Lama into exile in India (1959) many Tibetans had to leave their country. Up to now many Tibetans have undergone a difficult and dangerous flight through the Himalayas every year. Today approximately 130,000 Tibetan refugees live in exile, among them about 100,000 in India and Nepal, over 6,000 in more distant countries (primarily in Bhutan, Switzerland and the USA). With the generous support of a guest country - India - and many other supporters from all over the world the Tibetans in exile have managed to create their own new way of life in a relatively short time. In particular, they have managed to establish a well-developed education and training system and to create an important basis for preserving their culture. The main principle for the Tibetans in exile up to now has been their non-violent striving to return to their homeland and to live there in the freedom to determine their own lives.

Today there are also many children among the refugees. About 7,000 children have risked their lives crossing the Himalayas since the early 80s. According to the registrations by the office of UNHCR (United Nations High Commissioner for Refugees) in Kathmandu during the past few years, there are many small refugee children coming accompanied every year. During the strenuous trips through the Himalayas, taking several weeks, many children suffer from frostbite, and many drown while trying to cross rapid rivers. A considerable number of them go missing during the escape.

Many children and young people are sent by their families to Dharamsala, the seat of the Tibetan government in exile in northern India, to get a good basic education which corresponds to their culture and at the same time to the demands of modern education.

At present about 28,000 refugee children in exile are attending 87 Tibetan schools[4]. Owing to the big influx of the newcomers all children's villages and schools for the exiles are permanently overcrowded[5].

13

[4] Cf. Jetsun Pema: Tibetische Kinderdörfer, in Bernstorff, Dagmar /von Welck, Hubertus (ed.): *Tibet im Exil* (Baden-Baden, 2002) p.236
[5] On the whole there is relatively little reliable information about the Tibetan community in exile. Ethnological research took place in the 60s and has almost completely stopped since the 70s.

3. THE TIBETAN EDUCATION SYSTEM IN EXILE[6]

3.1. Education system in Tibet[7]

Before 1959 in Tibet there were hardly any public schools. Whereas the monasteries provided education to their novices and monks (at that time about 25% of the male population), privileged families employed private teachers, who taught their children at home.

Today, for a number of reasons, the education level of the Tibetans in Tibet is low. In many remote areas there are no schools, and many parents prefer not to send their children to boarding schools, mainly because they are not in a position to pay the high fees set by the Chinese government. The Chinese law on general compulsory education of 1986 says that every child from the age of seven should go to school, but there is also one clause which allows Tibetan children to postpone school entering until the age of nine. This is because there are many areas in Tibet where the infrastructure is underdeveloped and in which it is not possible to follow the full legal requirements.

3.2. The suppression of the Tibetan language

The Tibetan language policy is one of the most important topics in the education sector in Tibet, especially since the short period of liberalisation in the 80s. In July 1988 the Tibetan language was declared the official language of the autonomous republic of Tibet, but recent political measures have shown that this status has only a nominal value. In reality the Tibetan language is being supplanted more and more by Mandarin Chinese (the "national language" of the population of China).

For the Tibetans their mother tongue is the basis of their traditional culture. While teaching in the Tibetan language is allowed in some village schools, Chinese is used as the preferred language of teaching in the schools with the best equipment and the best teachers.

In the past few years in Tibet the extinction of the Tibetan language has speeded up, with widespread unemployment among Tibetan teachers, few translations of publications into Tibetan and the gradual disappearance of Tibetan as a language of communication. These are some of the factors that are accelerating the decline of the Tibetan language culture. Language researchers warn that young Tibetans already have problems in communicating with their older relatives. They thus become in a sense "aliens" in their own community. It is above all the written Tibetan language that is suffering from a drastic decline, and even educated Tibetans are gradually losing the ability to write their own language fluently.

[6] Cf. in: Tsepak Rigzin "Modernitat und Uberlieferung: Das tibetische Schulwesen." In: Bernstorff/von Welck, pp. 215ff

[7] Cf. in: "Das Bildungswesen in Tibet" Working document for the special rapporteur of the UN, Tibetan Centre for Human Rights and Democracy, www.tchrd.org, International Campaign for Tibet, Europe, June 2003-11-20

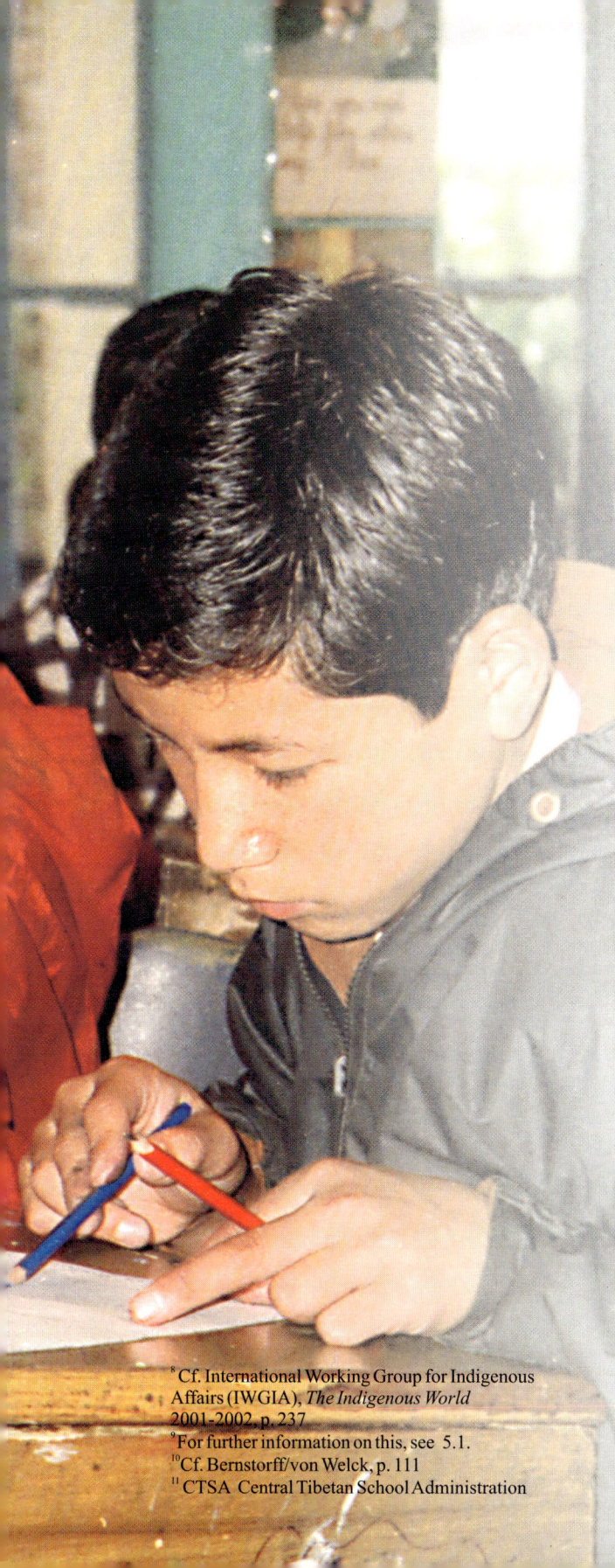

3.3. Tibetan education in exile

Over half of the refugees who seek asylum in India are children under 18 years old. 715 children most of them in the age group of 7-13-year-olds reached a reception centre in Dharamsala in 2002[8]. The under-aged, those who make dangerous and sometimes even fatal trips through the Himalayas, flee first of all in order to be able to attend Tibetan schools in exile and obtain a comprehensive and multi-faceted education. The parents entrust their children to unknown people (the so called guides) and give them money for this. The children arriving in India receive free education of high quality in the wide network of schools of various different types, established by His Holiness the Dalai Lama and the Tibetan government in exile all over the country.

3.4. Education in the monasteries

A certain proportion of Tibetan children are taught in the monasteries. Although the monasteries in general cannot be regarded as institutions of higher secondary education in the modern educational sense, up to now they have formed the pillars of the spiritual tradition in Tibet. They have certain features that correspond to modern educational practice, such as the awarding of grades. The Tibetans have always considered their monastic institutions as valuable places of education[9].

Within two generations the Tibetan community in exile managed to increase the education level from 25% to 70% of the population (including monks). For the age group of 15-19 it reached 97%. The girls from this age group today have the same education level as the boys.

The Department of Education of the Tibetan government in exile is in charge of schools for Tibetan refugee children and for the development of the education system in general. At present there are 87 Tibetan schools with 30,000 children, in India, Nepal and Bhutan, run by the Department of Education[10].

The schools are divided into four groups:
1) schools which are governed by the Central Tibetan School Administration[11] in New Delhi and are subject to the Indian Ministry of Education;
2) schools which are run and financed by the Department of Education of the central Tibetan government;
3) autonomous schools (belonging to the "Tibetan children villages", see below);
4) independent schools, which are run by foundations or private institutions.

15

[8] Cf. International Working Group for Indigenous Affairs (IWGIA), *The Indigenous World* 2001-2002, p. 237
[9] For further information on this, see 5.1.
[10] Cf. Bernstorff/von Welck, p. 111
[11] CTSA Central Tibetan School Administration

The link between modern education and the old Tibetan culture enables children to hold on to their traditional values and at the same time to develop a modern cosmopolitan attitude to life. They learn to be proud of their origin and culture, and at the same time they acquire technical and professional knowledge that will later help them to assert themselves in an increasingly tough and competition-oriented world.

3.5. Tibetan Children Villages (TCV)

Care for the Tibetan refugee children began in 1960 under the supervision of Tsering Dolma Takla (sister of the 14th Dalai Lama) when a home, the Nursery for Tibetan Refugee Children, was established. Since her death the work has been continued by her younger sister Jetsun Pema, who presides over the organisation that runs the Tibetan Children's Villages. The TCVs consist of a number of villages and autonomous schools. They form integrated communities and function as charitable institutions caring for orphans, semi-orphans and poor Tibetan children in exile. The financing is provided by the SOS-Children's Village-Foundation (49%), other organisations and sponsors (45%), and the government in exile (6%).

The children live under the care of Tibetan foster-parents. Besides the main hostel, situated in Dharamsala, there are a number of TCVs spread all over India. At present there are over 11,000 children in the TCVs and the institutions belonging to them, such as day-schools and care centres.

Jetsun Pema outlined as follows the original objectives of the Tibetan Children Village organisation, which are still valid today:
- *to care for the physical, intellectual and spiritual needs of the children;*
- *to impart the best of modern education and at the same time a fundamental understanding of the rich cultural traditions of Tibet;*
- *to develop national pride and identity and to help the children to share the hopes and efforts of the Tibetan people in returning to Tibet;*
- *to help the children to become independent and useful members of our society and of the whole human community*[12].

In the conversation that I held with her in 2002 Jetsun Pema made the following observations:
From a young age our children learn to behave compassionately towards all living beings. This is a part of our Buddhist religion. It is deeply rooted in the consciousness of the children.

In order to produce fully conscious human beings it is very important to provide children with an education emphasising values. This education imparts values that are based on our own culture and at the same time it is open to innovations.

Children learn from models. That which we as adults do is passed on to our children. In a society in which parents, teachers, in fact all members try to live with each other in harmony and peace, children can really believe in non-violence...

Likewise for her deputy Tsewang Yeshi the main aim of successful education lies in the ethical domain:

Education leads to a fundamental strengthening of the individual.
Our main aim is to form a good human being, that is:
- *one who thinks about others*
- *one who helps others*
- *one whose foremost concern is to serve the welfare of society and other human beings.*

---

[12] Cf. Pema, Jetsun , *Tibetan Children's Village.* Information brochure (Archana, 1996).

4. CREATIVE WORK WITH CHILDREN: DESCRIPTION OF THE METHODOLOGY

As was mentioned at the beginning, the central aim of this book is to provide insight into the inner world of Tibetan refugee children, their problems, wishes and hopes, by means of their pictures and written compositions. This strongly individual approach is designed help us share intensively the feelings of the children and to empathise with them in their situation.

Children painting and writing

Almost all children are motivated to express themselves in creative painting. In this way they give us, in symbolic form, access to the world of their thoughts. The special feature of the methodology used in this book is to link painting with writing and to develop ways of stimulating their imagination.

With the help of many teachers, private individuals and institutions all over the world, I have been collecting children's pictures and stories from different cultures for over 10 years. This has resulted in an extensive collection from more than thirty countries[13]. As this collection demonstrates, children do not always depict or write about joyful and carefree things. Rather, they express a wide range of their own feelings in diverse ways. Having looked through over 3,000 works from 30 countries, two tendencies become clear:

- Children from all over the world express similar feelings, such as fear of being left alone or abandoned, anxiety about environmental disasters and wars, or the wish for security, love and understanding.
- Specific cultural elements are present in many of the works.

During the course of this work, I found that again and again it was the children with particularly difficult fates, such as refugee children, who stood out. Apparently writing and painting were often the only possibility for these children to express their own experiences outwardly. It appears that deep-reaching traumatic experiences, such as the loss of homeland, family and mother tongue, can be expressed, and to some extent processed, through one's own writing and *Gestalt* images. Furthermore these works help us to project ourselves into the children's inner world of feelings and to empathise with them in their fate.

The search for their own roots appears to be a central theme. Especially children with traumatic experiences demonstrate again and again, through their pictures and writing, a strong need to deal with this important issue.

[13] The book "Fantasien von Kindern aus aller Welt"/"Fantasies of the children from all over the world", an intercultural reader and picture-book, appeared in 1998 as the first larger publication in the framework of the collection, in which children formulated their fantasies in pictures and writings. The work with the children shows how personality and cultural variables can lead to the stimulating perspective changes (Rabkin, G. et al. "Fantasien von Kindern aus aller Welt", Stuttgart 1998)

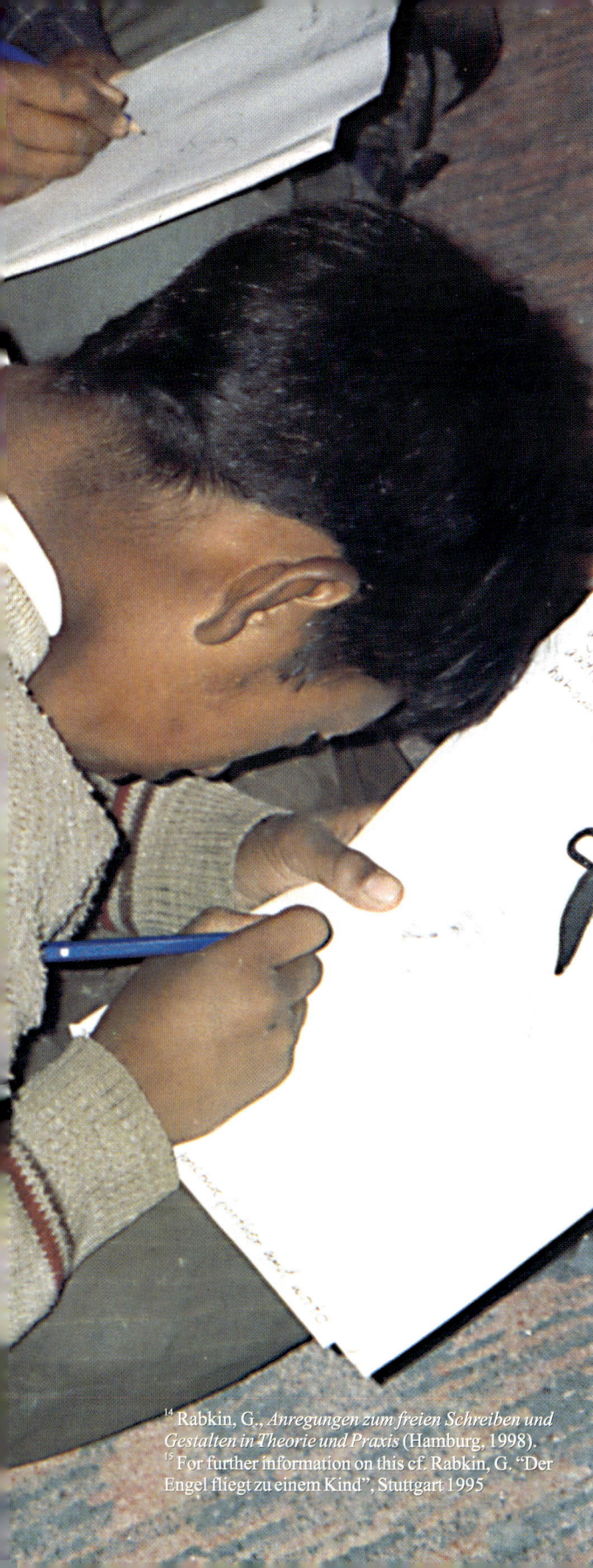

The project "Creativity, Culture and Basic Education": developing stimuli to creative writing and painting

The collection of children's pictures is the basis and starting point of an international cooperation project of the UNESCO Institute for Education and the Department of Education and Sport of the Free and Hanseatic City of Hamburg called "Creativity, Culture and Basic Education Non-conventional Ways to Writing and Culture[14].

This project, informed by the approach I have just described, has pursued the overall aim of enabling the children to express their own feelings and thoughts, opening up for them the world of writing and giving them access to the cultures of the world.

Using this concept, whose theoretical roots come from the holistic and Gestalt psychology of the Leipzig school, various stimuli to free writing and creation were conceived[15], by means of which great creative potential can be released. The use of stimuli to free writing and image creation is intended to motivate children to express their emotions and to embark on a process of self-understanding. The stimuli are meant to encourage them to create their own gestalt images and forms, without too much pre-structuring, and to begin to give shape to their inner processes through pictures and writing.

When using these stimuli, it is always the visual aspect that is presented first, followed by the written aspect. The task is always the same and is always intentionally formulated in the following simple words:

Carry on painting the picture, and write a story about it!

The opportunity to elaborate a picture and then to write something under it, helps children gradually to feel their way into their own imaginative processes. At first they will experience some gaps that need explanation, and they will feel the urge to work things out in writing.

At all stages of the work no instructions are given from outside - this means no previous common interpretation of the pictures and no instructions relating to pictures and texts. The work is interrupted only if some questions arise which need clarification.

Different forms of stimuli

One way to work with the stimuli to free writing and creation is to motivate children to give expression to their own thoughts through interaction with the works of art. Thus, through interacting with art they learn to develop self-understanding

In practice it turned out in the course of time that semi-abstract pictures by classical modern artists are especially suitable for the development of one's own ideas, because they have a certain open,

19

[14] Rabkin, G., *Anregungen zum freien Schreiben und Gestalten in Theorie und Praxis* (Hamburg, 1998).
[15] For further information on this cf. Rabkin, G. "Der Engel fliegt zu einem Kind", Stuttgart 1995

dynamic quality that allows the children to give free rein to their own fantasies. They motivate the viewers to go beyond the literal pictorial content and to express their own individual, often very varied, ideas. Such works include, for example, pictures and sketches by Pablo Picasso and Paul Klee. In general, all works are appropriate which allow more than one interpretation. Incomplete sketches by earlier painters are also suitable, since they have a similar open quality that can act as a motivation to one's own further creation (for example, sketches by Leonardo da Vinci, Michelangelo or Rembrandt). The choice is, of course, not limited to western art but can include works from all over the world, such as African sculptures, Japanese Hokusai woodcuts or pictures by the Mexican painter Frida Kahlo. The present project, for example, used many works from the Tibetan-Buddhist culture. The stimuli to free writing and creation come not only from the fine arts, but can include geometrical forms or objects that stimulate different senses, such as touch, hearing and smell[16].

The children's works are reflections of their social environment and draw attention to the problems with which they are faced. The imaginative images that they create act as projections of their individual feelings.

20

[16] Cf.: Rabkin, G. "Die schöne Hexe", Stuttgart 2000

5. CREATIVE WORK WITH TIBETAN CHILDREN LIVING IN EXILE

My search for Tibetan children in their places of exile and my creative work with them took me to the following locations:

Kathmandu, Nepal (March, 1998);
Ulan-Ude, Buryatia (Ivolginsk monastery) (summer 1998);
Rikon, Switzerland (October 1998, March 1999);
Hamburg Germany;
Leh, Ladakh (audience with His Holiness the Dalai Lama), TCV (May 1999);
Dharamsala, India, TCV (July 2000, March 2001, March 2002, March 2003, March 2004).

Every trip was different and turned out to be a very personal way to develop friendships and many stimulating contacts. My initial idea developed further during fruitful discussions in the field in the course of these trips. Therefore, as I recount these trips chronologically I shall also include some personal observations. This presentation of my experiences does not lay any claim to completeness. Rather it is a kaleidoscope of impressions. Above all, it is the thoughts and works of the children that are the central theme.

In some places I not only made contact with the Tibetan children, but also had a chance to communicate with the people from their community. All this began with a trip to Kathmandu where, in the hotel where I stayed, I got to know one Tibetan, who helped me through his "network" to gain my initial access into the world of the Tibetans in exile and to work in many monasteries with child novices.

One of the larger groups of the Tibetan refugee children that I encountered was in the Swiss village of Rikon in the Tösstal, not far from Zurich. In my home town of Hamburg there are only a few Tibetans residing.

The focus of my work with children was in Dharamsala, which is at the same time the seat of the Tibetan government in exile. All in all I have been there five times and was able to work at that time with many children in the TCV. Over the whole period I was able to work with the same children continuously and thus had a chance to follow their development.

My trip to Ladakh was of special importance, because there I had a chance to present my project to His Holiness, the 14th Dalai Lama during a private audience.

The trip to Ulan-Ude in Siberia brought me not to the Tibetan but to the Buryat novices, who are now allowed once again to receive a monastic education in the Tibetan Buddhist tradition since the opening of Russia. A special chapter is devoted to my work with them, and they were the focus of other trips to Buddhists in Russia (Moscow, July 1999. St. Petersburg, 2002 and 2003). In the following pages these separate trips are described briefly in their chronological order.

far away from home

5.1. Kathmandu, Nepal
The situation of Tibetan exiles in Nepal

Because of its geographical position Nepal has played a key role since 1959 as an escape route, transit area and country of refuge for the Tibetans[17].

Depending on the starting place in Tibet, the trip to the Tibetan-Nepalese border can take weeks or months. Most Tibetan refugees cross the high terrain of the Himalayas by frequently used escape paths. They usually go via Nangpa-la-Pass, which separates Tibet from Nepal. Children and adolescents make up about one third of the newcomers.

In 1991 UNHCR[18] opened an office in Kathmandu and began to register the Tibetans who had fled from Tibet as "endangered people". Since then an average of 2,500 Tibetans have applied to UNHCR for protection every year, although in some years the number has been considerably higher.

The mandate of UNHCR in Kathmandu regarding the newcomers from Tibet is to secure their status as "endangered people", to register them and to facilitate a quick and safe transit through Nepal. UNHCR considers Tibetans in Nepal first of all as refugees who are to be protected. However, there are also groups that fall into a grey zone for UNHCR. These include numerous religious pilgrims and parents who have the aim of bringing their small children to India to obtain a school education. Although theoretically these people do not fall under the definition of refugees, UNHCR tries to be as useful as possible for them.

Some Tibetans stay in Nepal, many go further to Dharamsala, as well as to Switzerland or other countries.

The road to Kathmandu and the novices

When I set off for Kathmandu in March 1998 with Valery Bugrov and two Russian acquaintances, Ludmila and Volodya, I had just finished my dissertation while working full-time as lecturer at the Institute for In-Service Teacher Training in Hamburg. I was in an exhausted and privately confused state and was looking for something new. An unfulfilled dream of mine was to work with a group that had always interested me, namely Tibetan refugee children living in exile in different parts of the world.

After my arrival in Kathmandu at the hotel Vajra , located outside the noisy city centre and built in the Tibetan style, I had at first no idea how I could get closer to my aim. Next day I happened to get into conversation with Sonam Wangchuk, a young Tibetan who was working as an intern at the hotel reception before beginning his studies in hotel management. I explained to him that Valeriy, Ludmila and Volodya wanted to go on a trekking tour in the Himalayas, and that I was dreaming about working with Tibetan children.

"Classroom" on the roof of the monastery

22

[17] Cf. in: International Campaign for Tibet Germany (ICT), *Gefährliche Flucht bedingungen tibetischer Flüchtlinge* (updated 2002), Germany 2003, p.1ff

[18] UNHCR office of the United Nations High Commissioner for Refugees (The UN High Commissioner for Refugees protects and supports millions of refugees all over the world).

No problem. Sonam made a swaying movement with his head and - for a moment - it was not clear for me whether it meant yes or no, but within a few hours, thanks to Sonam, our wishes were coming within sight of realisation. I had experienced my first encounter with the pragmatic and energetic organisational skill of a Tibetan.

Sonam and his friends organised everything necessary for the Russians to make a five-day trip to Pokhara, with tents and adventurous cooking arrangements. Sonam wanted to accompany me and to see various Tibetan Buddhist monasteries with which he had personal contacts and in which I could later work with the Tibetan novices who had fled from Tibet to Nepal and were being brought up in the monasteries.

The three Russians visited a small shop for trekking equipment and fitted themselves out as though they were about to climb Mount Everest, buying equipment for a five-person team including bearers, a guide and a cook. After their departure I was able to concentrate on my own plans.

Work with the novices of the Karma-Raja-Maha-Vihar monastery

23

In Nepal there are many Tibetan children growing up in Tibetan-Buddhist monasteries, and they include a large number of orphans and refugees. The monasteries in exile make an important contribution to preserving the Tibetan culture through their schools and universities, their libraries and hand-craft studios. Creating a settled way of life for the Tibetan monks and nuns involves great economic difficulties. Although the clergy try as best they can to take care of the settlements on their own, it is always necessary to find donations from abroad. The monasteries often get money from sponsors and from public funds, and they earn some income from small-scale commercial activities, such as running small restaurants or shops on the premises and offering tourist accommodation.

The monastery schools work independently, that is to say without any state control by the Nepalese Ministry of Education. Accommodation and teaching costs are carried by the monasteries. Parents are not charged for their children's education there.

Instruction in the monastery is arranged according to the four traditional methods (imitating, learning by heart, explaining and debating). A pupil is put into the next learning group when he or she is "ready" for this (here "readiness" does not necessarily correspond to age or achievements). There are no marks. When a child fails in an exam he goes on learning until he passes. Much work is done in groups where younger and older pupils are mixed together.

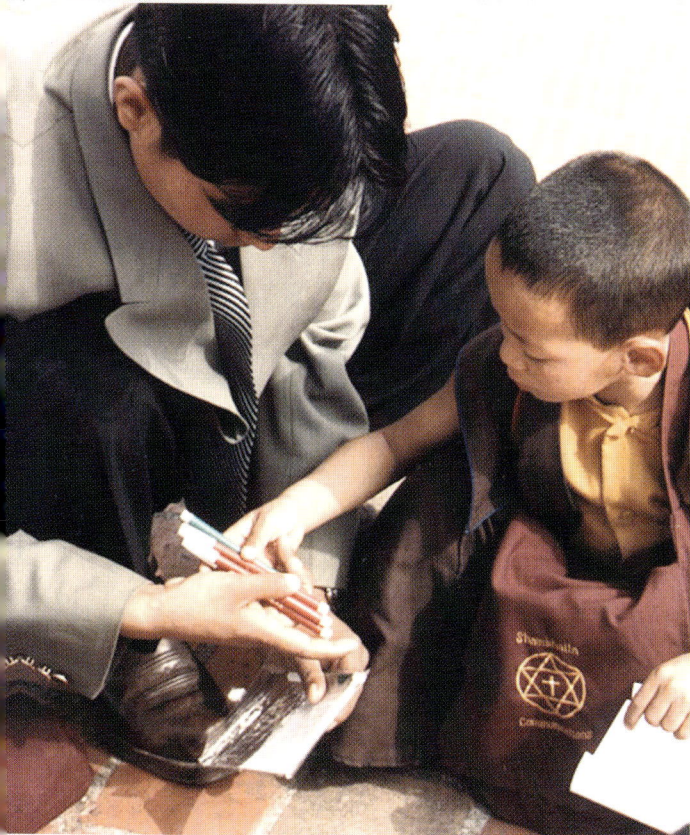

Sonam Wangchuk with Karma Rinchen

Sonam first arranged a visit to the Karma-Raja-Maha-Vihar monastery for me. It was situated a short walking distance from my hotel, but first one had to climb many steps to reach the top of the hill where the Stupa[19], the monastery and other buildings were located. Passing beggars and souvenir traders, we came closer to the enormous Vajra, and the SwayambuNath-Stupa[20] loomed up in front of us. A few metres to the left was "our" monastery, the Karma-Raja-Maha-Vihar. It is the second Tibetan monastery which has been set up outside the country since the occupation of Tibet and it belongs to Kagyu-tradition[21]. The monastery has its own school with one classroom for the children of all age groups. There are about 20 pupils and a teacher for younger monks (about 7 to 12 years old).

The daily routine of a monk-pupil

5.00:	getting-up and performing *puja*[22]
8.00:	breakfast
9.00-11.00:	reading and writing (English, Nepali)
11.30:	lunch
Up to 14.00:	free time
14.00-15.00:	*puja*
15.00:	reading and writing (Tibetan)
17.30:	dinner
19.00-20.00:	stupa circling
20.30	sleep

The daily routine described above makes it clear that generally two hours a day are spent in prayers and three hours in other lessons (language instruction in Tibetan, English and Nepali). The curriculum for Tibetan studies in this school consists of Tibetan grammar, history and religious literature. The books used differ from monastery to monastery. Mathematics - unlike in other monasteries is not taught here. Lessons also take place on Sundays. Only Saturdays are free from lessons.

24

[19] *Stupa*: sacred building. It is a religious ritual in Tibetan Buddhism to go round the Stupa clockwise.
[20] *SwayambuNath-Stupa* is one of the biggest shrines of Tibetan Buddhism. It dates back to the year 410 AD.
[21] In Tibetan Buddhism there are four main traditions: *Kagyu, Nyingma, Sakya and Geluk.*
[22] *Puja*: a prayer

KARMA

KARMADUPGYUE

The Himalaya Mountains (free painting)
Karma Dupgyue, 10 years old,
Karma-Raja-Vihar monastery, Kathmandu

DUPGYUE

They are already expecting us. When the weather is dry (and not too cold) lessons take place on the roof of the monastery. A marvellous view over the SwayambuNath-Stupa, the entire valley and the majestic snow-covered mountains of the Himalayas opens before us.

A mixed-age group of 7-14-year-old novices is waiting for us. It is good that Sonam and I had obtained crayons, paper and of course sweets in advance. Evidently, apart from the holy texts, the novices do not possess many study materials. We squat down on the floor and Sonam interprets my explanations.

The work goes without any problems, in a relaxed, cheerful and concentrated atmosphere. We come back several times and continue our work, take many photos and conduct interviews with the teacher and some of the children.

26

Three monks in their "classroom" on top of the roof
Karma-Raja-Vihar monastery, Kathmandu

The results of the work are presented

Karma Pasang, a monastery pupil in Kathmandu/Nepal, 10 years old

Karma Pasang has been living for about two years in the monastery. His family, who sent him to study at the monastery, emigrated from Tibet to Shabru in the Sindu-Palchok region of Nepal. Karma Pasang was born there. To go from his monastery school to the place where his family lives he has to make a trip of three days two days by bus and one day on foot.

There are nine family members: his father, mother, two sisters, three elder brothers, one younger brothers and himself. His father is a builder, his mother is a weaver. One of his elder brothers is also a monk. His other three brothers are still at school. His sisters have to work in the field.

The monastery of course plays a central role in his life. Karma Pasang feels at ease in the monastery. He says that he prefers living there to living at home. Later he would like to stay as a monk at the monastery. As for hobbies, he mentions reading books and playing football.

In his free, spontaneous paintings he is fond of depicting various scenes from his monastic environment with important details like a water fountain, Tibetan flags and especially the long, seemingly endless stairs leading up to the monastery. He shows them winding around the Swayambunath hill. In a number of other paintings he depicts religious motifs.

In his adaptation of Paul Klee's *Angel with a Little Bell* (1939), Karma Pasang illustrates a problem that he knows at first hand. He suffers - like many Tibetan children from a troublesome eye illness which comes back periodically[23]. On the day when he drew the picture and wrote the text his right eye was completely swollen.

28

[23] The widespread eye illness is possibly caused by the intensity of the sun's rays at a height of about 4,000 metres, besides heavy pollution of the environment (e.g. a high level of smoke in the air). Other unsatisfactory hygienic conditions also often cause eye infections.

Karma Pasang painting the monastery

Karma Pasang: Our monastery (free painting)

His name is "owl".
He cannot see during the day.
He can open his eyes only at night.

Karma Pasang, 11 years old
Original: Tibetan and English

In his story he finds at least a temporary solution to the problem of not being able to see properly. He interprets Paul Klee's angel as an owl. This is a bird that he can observe in the surroundings of his monastery at night. Karma Pasang knows that these animals *can open their eyes only at night.* He shows the owl's "clothing" in various shades of red. These colours as well as the form of the clothing are strongly reminiscent of his monk's garb. In this way he emphasises his sense of identification with the figure of the owl. Perhaps his identification with the owl is linked to an unconscious wish at least to be able to see well at night. In the realm of fantasy this is possible!

29

30

Nuns of Keydong nunnery painting and writing

Nuns of the Keydong nunnery Thuk Che-Choling in Kathmandu

After we had finished out visit to the Karma-Raja-Maha-Vihar monastery, we headed for the Keydong nunnery, Thuk Che-Choling, which has over 80 nuns. It lies at the foot of SwayambuNath hill and belongs to the Gelugpa tradition.

The atmosphere is friendly and open-minded. Freshly washed white khatas[24] and wine-red nun's gowns flutter in the spring wind. The abbess benevolently greeted us with a cat on her shoulder. After strong buttered tea in their office, we were led onto a kind of a terrace and there we were surrounded by a group of 12-14-year-old nuns who besieged Sonam with questions. It turned out that he had once given them an English lesson.

Sitting tightly together on the floor of the corridor in front of the rooms, they enthusiastically set about tackling the tasks we gave them. As the examples shown here demonstrate, many of their pictures and stories have religious or social themes.

31

[24]*Khata*: Tibetan ceremonial white silk scarf traditionally used for greetings and blessings

In her first story Tenzin Dhadon emphasises the social aspect of poverty and work under severe conditions, and in her second story she focuses on religious themes.

Her parents live in India, a three-day bus journey away. Her parents are peasants, and her brothers and sisters go to a village school. Only once every three years can she be visited by her family. Her main interest is religion. First she would like to become a good nun and later to set up her own nunnery. She likes her nunnery because it offers her good study prospects. In parallel she goes to Namgyal Middle boarding school. Her favourite subjects are Tibetan and English. In her free time she enjoys reading books and playing party games with others.

A story

Once there was a man. His name is Joseph.
He works daily.His work is cutting wood.
Per day he gets 50 rupies[25].
He is tired but he can't rest.
He thinks if he rests he doesnrt get much money.
He has only one dirty and damaged
shirt and trousers.
He has no friends and (family) members.
He has a small house[26].

Tenzin Dhadon, 14 years old
Original: Tibetan and English

32

[25] At the present exchange rate (March 2004) the Nepalese rupee corresponds to 0.01 Euro, about 1 Cent, i.e. 50 rupees correspond to half a Euro or 50 Cents!

[26] In all children's stories mistakes in English have been "cautiously" corrected (e.g. grammatical errors)

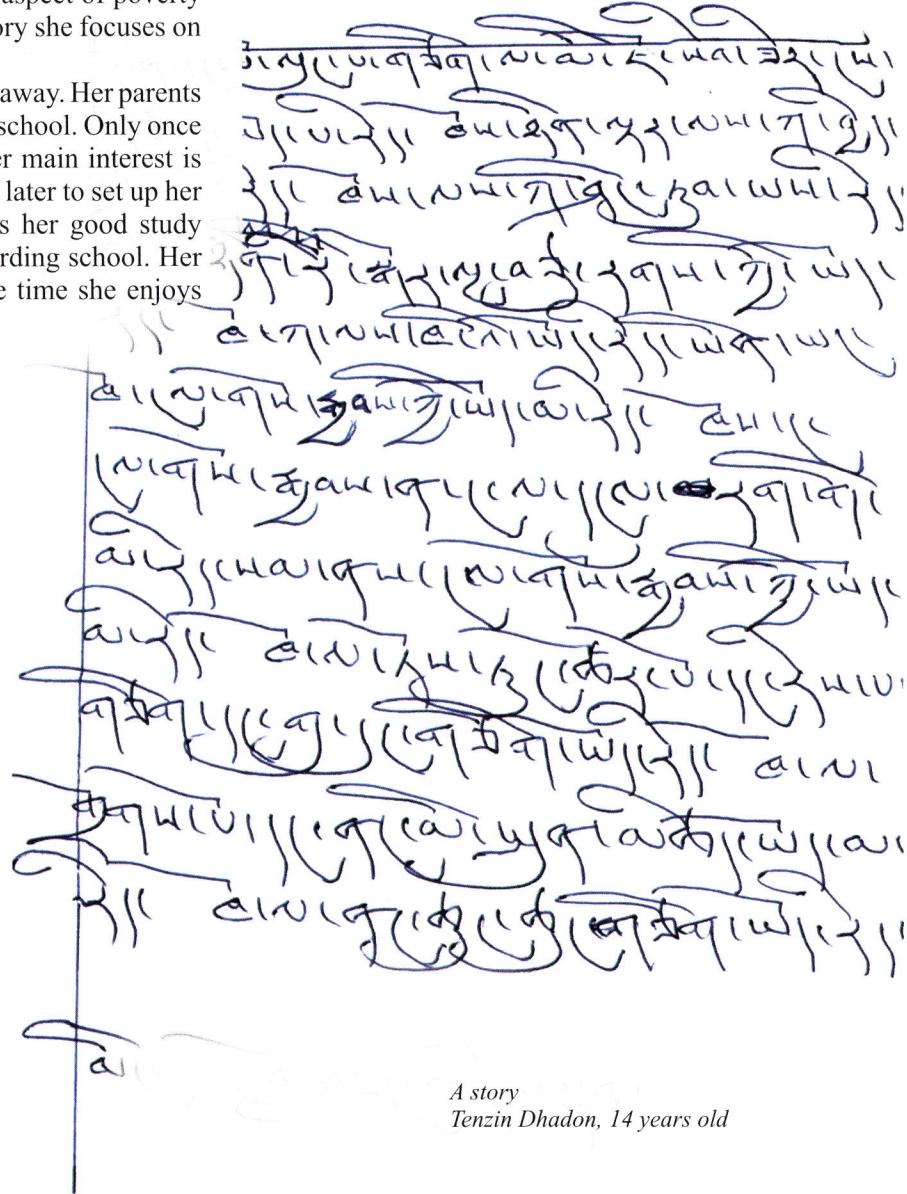

A story
Tenzin Dhadon, 14 years old

A Story

Once upon there is a man. His name is Joseph. He work's daily. His work is cutting wood. Per day he get's 50 rupees. He is tired but he can't rest. He think, if he rest he didn't get much money. He had only one dirty and damage shirt and trouser. He had no friends and members also. He has a small house.

Sisyphus, from the Hamburg artists' group. Die Schlumper

His name is Lobsang

He is a religious minded boy.
He gets up early in the morning
and prostrates before breakfast.
He loves God and his family.

Tenzin Dhadon, 14 years old
Original: English

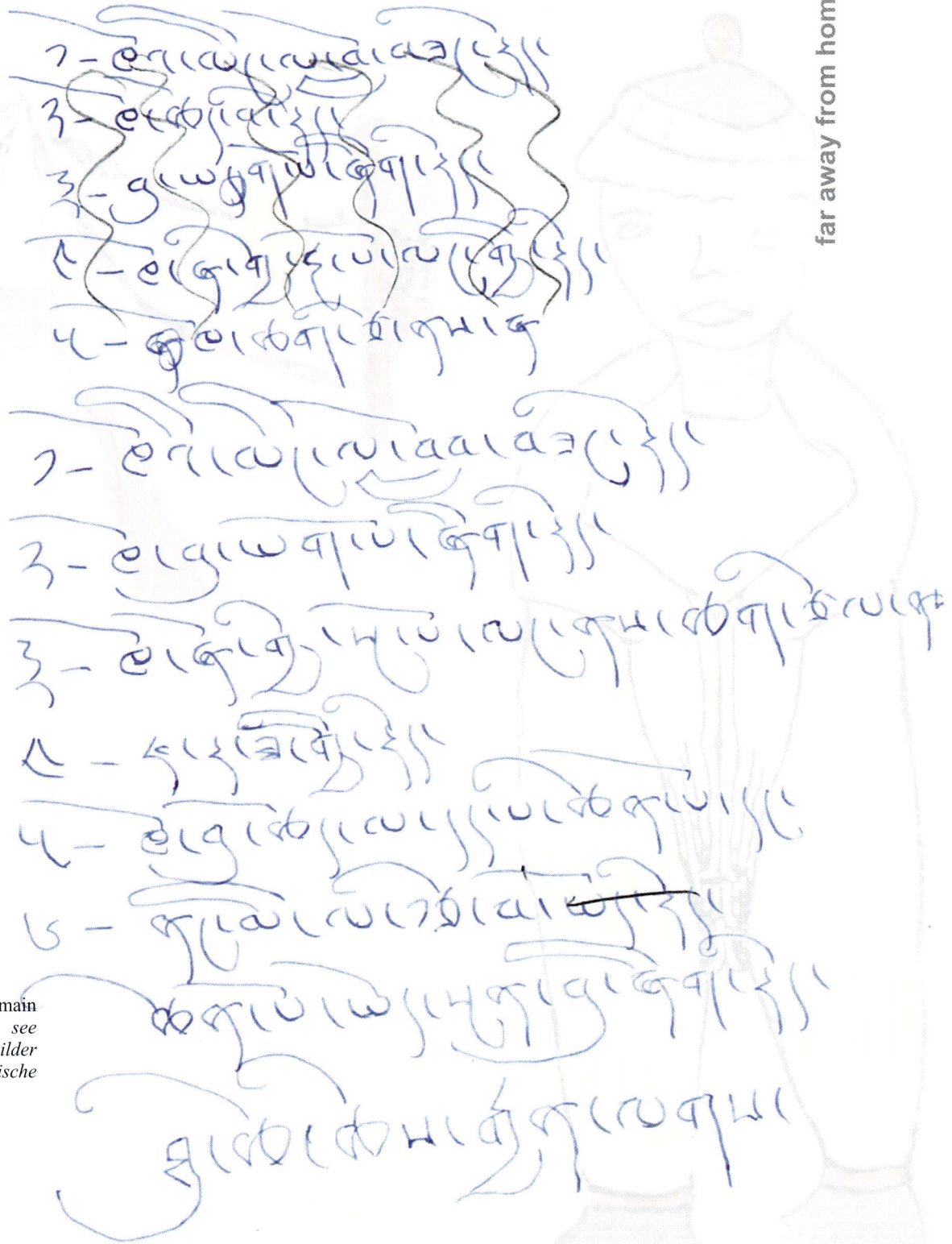

34

His name is Lobsang
Tenzin Dhadon, 14 years old

For the symbolic meaning of the main hand positions (Sanskrit: *mudra*) *see* Alexandra Lavizzari-Raeuber. *Rollbilder aus dem Himalaya - Kunst und mystische Bedeutung"* (89), pp 97 ff

SWOYAMBHU STUPA

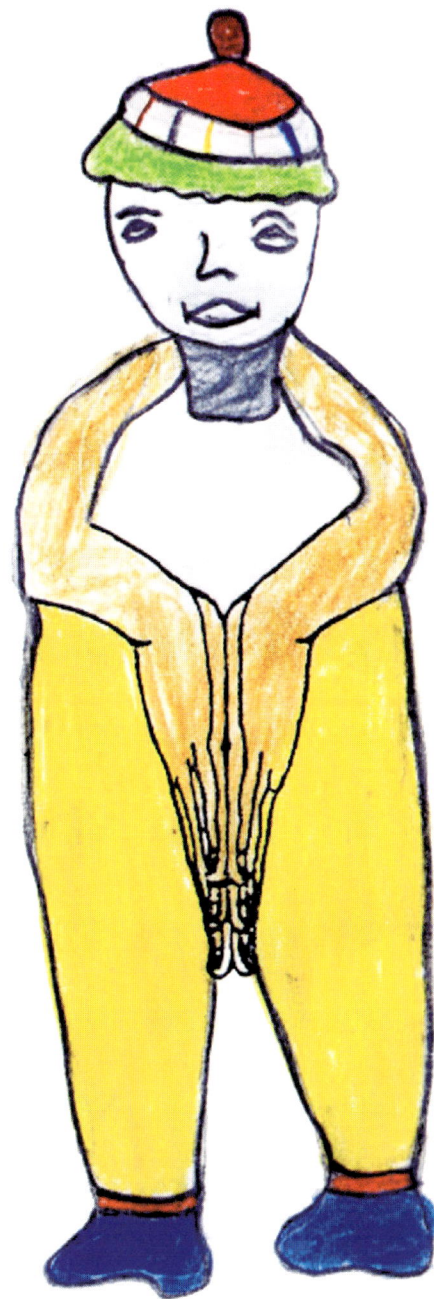

His name is lobsang. He is religious minded boy. He gets up early in the morning and prostrates before breakfast. He loves to god and his family.

A sign board
This is a sign board of this village.
Its smile means happiness because all the people live
happily here.
Its big ears symbolise that the people here receive many news on
radio, television and from newspapers.
There all the people are very intelligent!

Thupten Gakey, 12 years old, Kathmandu, Nepal
Original: Tibetan

Thupten Gakey's parents live in India, but she does not visit them. She does not yet have any concrete plans for the future. At the moment she would like to be a nun. In her first story Thupten Gakey creates various symbolic meanings. She interprets the wide smile of the figure in the original picture as a sign of happiness. She sees the large ears as signifying the use of mass media or, alternatively, as a sign of open-mindedness and intelligence.

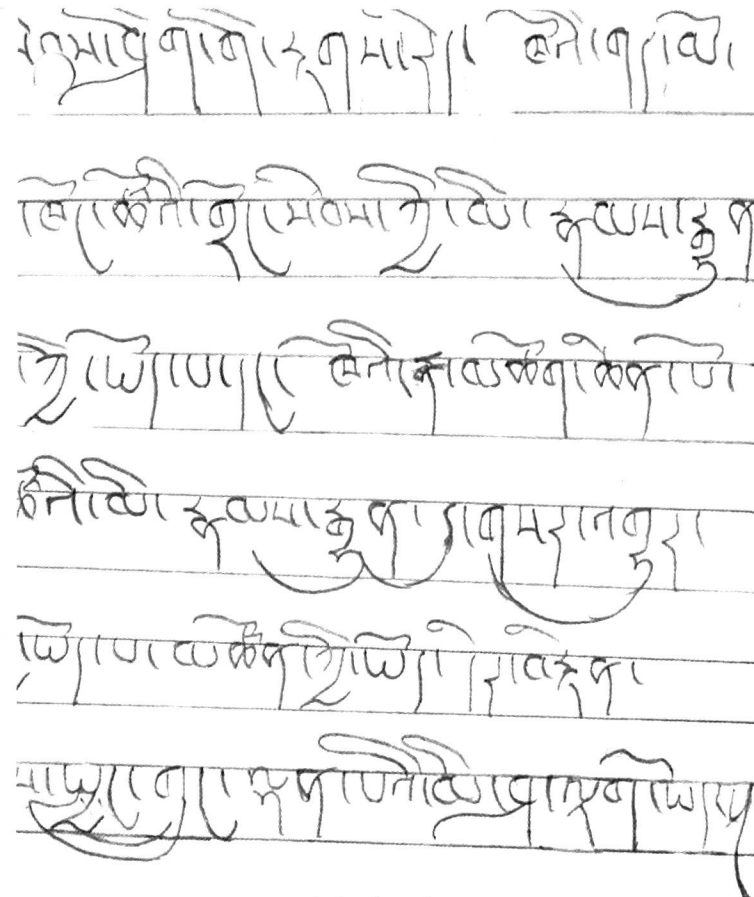

36

Once there lived a beautiful girl in the country[27]
She had only one flaw: her face.
Her hair was very beautiful.
All the people loved her hair.
Her favourite colour was pink and she liked all colourful things.
She cannot see things clearly, that's why she wears glasses.

Thupten Gakey, 14 years old (two years later), Kathmandu, Nepal
Original: English

In her second story she also tries to discover what certain features of the face could mean. Here she is possibly also reflecting her own needs. Particularly striking is her admiration for nice hair (which they as nuns are not allowed to have) and colourful clothes (which for the nuns are limited to shades of red).

A sign board
Thupten Gakey, 12 years old

[27] From Paul Klee, *Senecio*

Treppensteiger (stair climbers), from the
Hamburg artists' group *Die Schlumper*

LOBSANG

Lobsang Chokey also chooses a religious topic. She describes a familiar Buddhist ritual and at the same time a much respected person who has an important role in her life: the abbess.

The seat of our abbess
This is our abbess`seat.
She always gets up early in the morning and prays for god.
During the prayer she uses a bell and Vajra which sounds very nice
and gives peace in the mind and body.
We, nuns, also use them.

Lobsang Chokey, 13 years old, Kathmandu, Nepal
Original: English

38

My hobby is reading   (Keydong Nunnery)

My hobby is writing   (Keydong Nunnery)

A STORY

This is our abbess seat. she always gets up early in the morning and pray for gat. During prayer she uses bell and vajra which sounds very nice and give peace in the mind and body we nuns also use them.

From: Lavizarri-Raeuber (89)

CHOKEY

5.2. Special chapter: Buddhist novices in Buryatia

Buddhism in Buryatia[28]

Buryatia, a republic in the eastern part of the Russian Federation with Ulan-Ude as its capital, is situated on Lake Baikal. Buryatia is a region with a long Buddhist tradition (just as in the former Soviet regions of Tuva and Kalmukia.

Until 1917 there was an active exchange between Tibetan and Buryat Buddhists. For example Agwan Dordjieff, the teacher of the 13th Dalai Lama, was a Buryat. For over 50 years, starting in the 1930s, the 400-year-old tradition of Buryat Buddhism was interrupted owing to the dominant policies of the Soviet Union at that time. Out of the 47 previously active monasteries (datsan), not a single one still survived at the beginning of the 20th century, and even the memory of these places had partly disappeared. Many Lamas fled to Tibet. The Buryat population suffered greatly from the policy of enforced atheism, and one third of them were murdered. Only after perestroika did it become possible for Buryatia to resume its religious traditions openly. At present Buryatia is experiencing a rebirth of Buddhism. Important support is given by the 14th Dalai Lama.

A trip to Buryatia

Hamburg - Kaliningrad - Moscow - Irkutsk - Ulan-Ude - that was my itinerary in July 1998.

First we stayed overnight in Zelenogorsk (formerly the East Prussian town of Rauschen) not far from Kaliningrad, built on steep cliffs facing the Baltic. The next night we stayed with a friend in Moscow. He lived in grand style in the former apartment of an admiral who had belonged to the Nomenclature and whose granddaughter earned a considerable extra income from the extremely high rent. Nearly everything in the flat remained as it was 50 years earlier: carefully restored inlaid furniture, valuable porcelain and other choice items. I browsed in the admiral's extensive library and found works by Pasternak, Bulgakov, and Mandelstam all in Russian editions from the Soviet period! In the evening Valery took me to dine at a splendid hotel not far from the Kremlin. Accompanied by Balalaika music, we ate traditional Russian delicacies at sinfully high prices. As we left the place there was an unbelievably large full moon shining over the towers of the Kremlin. The following day we started our trip to Irkutsk.

[28] CF. WWW.ROLFKLEIN.DE/BURATIEN.HTML

In Irkutsk time seems to run differently. Siberia, with its seemingly endless distances, seemed to me almost unchanged since the Soviet era. We paddled in Lake Baikal and ate fresh fish caught in the lake and grilled by the roadside. The trans-Siberian railway, by which we covered the last stretch from Irkutsk to Ulan-Ude along Lake Baikal, was the same as when I saw it for the first time in the 1970s.

At last we arrived in Ulan-Ude. Over 350,000 inhabitants live in the capital of Buryatia. Among the colourful mixture of nationalities, the Buryat represent only a small part of the population, compared with the Russians. The city of Ulan-Ude is over 300 years old and therefore is one of the oldest towns in Siberia. I also found out that in the Soviet time hundreds of Buddhist *Thangkas*[29] and other Buddhist and Russian Orthodox relics were hidden in Odigitria cathedral, a baroque Russian Orthodox Church. Today the relics are on display in a newly opened historical museum of Ulan-Ude.

We stayed in a hotel whose standard of comfort was reminiscent of Soviet times but whose prices were distinctly western. The rain was pattering on the corrugated iron roof. I bought a small Buddha carved in cedar wood, which I discovered in a souvenir shop among colourfully painted matrioshkas and fur hats. Then we prepared to set off for the Buddhist monastery of Ivolginsk, situated about 35 kilometres from Ulan-Ude. As the bus trip was going to be complicated, Valery tried to rent a private car. Finally Valery appeared with the Russian owner of a grey Lada, who agreed to take us to Ivolginsk for an acceptable price. He was surprised that we wanted to go there, but he had already taken "two Lamas from abroad" to the monastery.

41

IVOLGINSK

Ivolginsk monastery

After about a one-hour ride through the slightly hilly steppe, passing villages with traditional Russian wooden houses, the golden-yellow roofs of the monastery lit up in the distance on the horizon. The entire monastery complex is separated from the surroundings by a high wooden fence. Our driver promised to wait for us. We waded through puddles, besieged by mosquitoes. In the main temple we met a Buryat woman, who was selling incense sticks and Buddhist scriptures (some of them in Cyrillic) in a kiosk. She listened patiently as I explained my reason for coming to the monastery, then she pointed at a wooden house. There lived Lama Oleg, who would certainly be able to help me.

Lama Oleg turned out to be a young Russian from Vladivostok, who had been living for some time with his small family in this simple house. It was very cosy inside, with a big Russian oven and carpets on the walls, but most of all I was struck by many Buddhist things: a small altar, *tangkas*, *khatas* and Buddhist Holy Scriptures. Lama Oleg seemed in no way surprised by our arrival and my request. He listened attentively to us and looked with great interest through the intercultural reading book *Children's' Fantasies from all over the World*.

Meanwhile we had been joined by a group of novices, who listened keenly to our conversation. Lama Oleg suggested that I should leave my materials there (working sheets and crayons) and come back in a few days. Sure enough, when we came back a few days later, feeling some apprehension, he and his novices presented us with some wonderful works which they had made and which strongly reflected their intensive study of Tibetan Buddhism.

The main temple of the Ivolginsk monastery

The entrance to the monastery (View from the monastery over kiosk and "our" Lada)

42

43

Aldar, Bajadschalai and Zirlin-Dascha are looking through the intercultural reader in the house of Lama Oleg   (Ivolginsk)

Энэ дэлхэйн барилдаанай урилдаанда түрүү hуури эзэлхэн Буряадай сууга барилдаашан Мунхэ-Бата гээшэ.

1. Story

44

This man is a wrestler.
He is on the first place in wrestling.
His name is Monhabat.

Bajadschalai, 17 years old, Ivolginsk monastery,
Buryatia
Original: Buryatian (in Cyrillic script)

1. Story
Bajadschalai, 17 years old
Treppensteiger (stair climbers),
from the Hamburg artists' group
Die Schlumper

Энэ лама Бурханда мургэжэ
байна. Орхы амитадай убшэн
зоболон дчы ябахын тула,
тиигээд Орхы амитадай буянтай
ута наратай удаан жаргалтай
ябахын тула залбирна.

2. Story
This Lama prays,
for the living beings not to suffer,
for all living beings to live long and happily.
Lord Buddha sits and meditates
in order to free all living beings from sufferings and illnesses.

Bajadschalai, 17 years old, Ivolginsk monastery, Buryatia
Original: Buryatian (in Cyrillic script)

2. Story
Bajadschalai, 17 years old (Ivolginsk)

ALDAR

Aldar comes from Kishingi in Buryatia and also created his text in Buryatian with Cyrillic writing. He is the youngest in his family and has three sisters. One day he also would like to become a lama and mostly plays football in his free time.

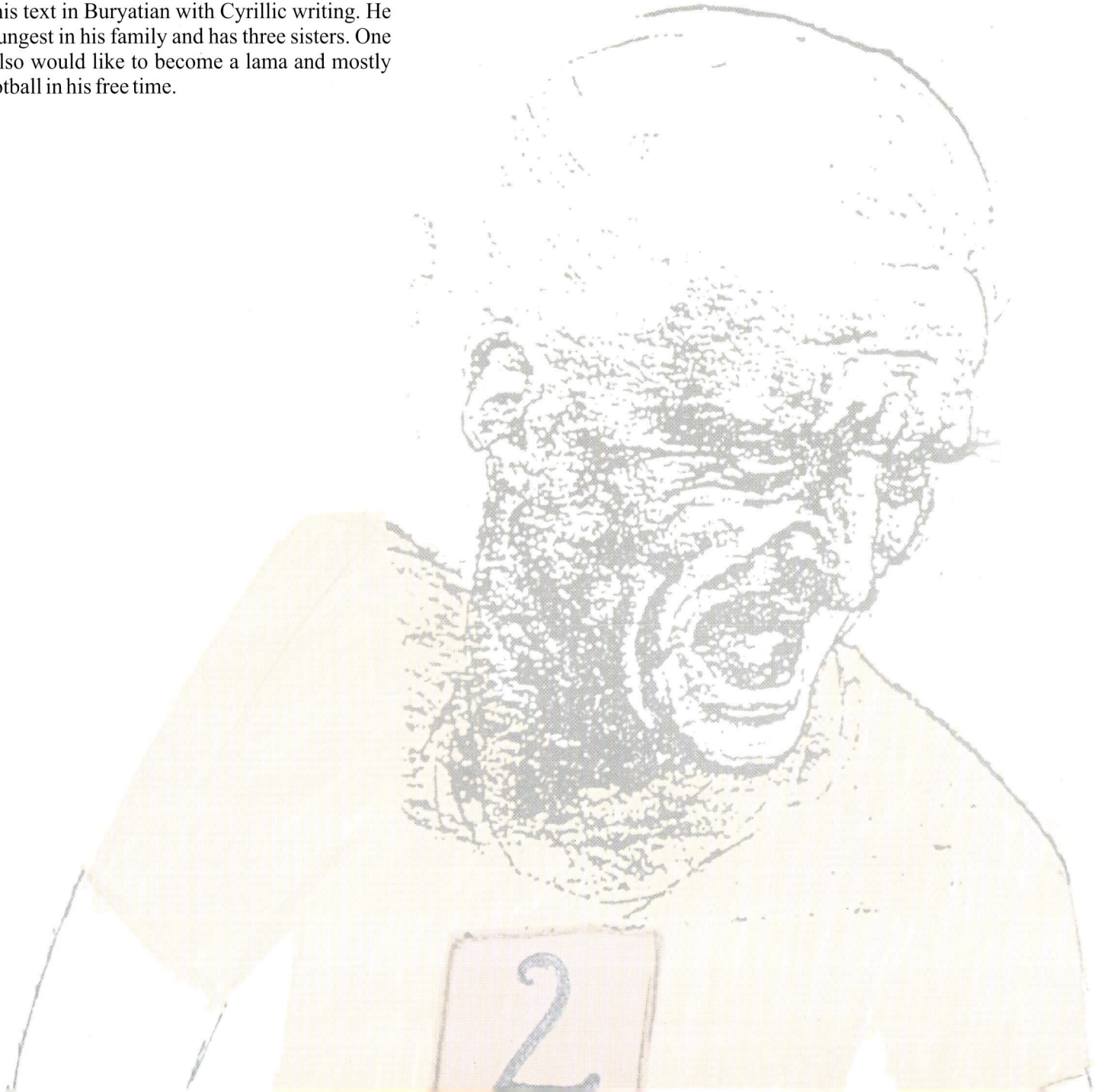

46

ИМЯ **Алдар**

ВОЗ РАСТ **13 лет**
АДРЕСС **г Улан-Удэ ул Соснова 6 кадезд 4 этаж 38кв**
ПОЖАЛУЙСТА, РИСУЙТЕ!
ПИШИТЕ ИСТОРИЮ!

Энэ хүн гол оруулжа hонона

This man would like to score a goal.
Aldar, 13 years old

Original: Buryatian (in Cyrillic script)
From Leonardo da Vinci , *Facial Studies*

We said a heartfelt goodbye to Oleg Lama and his novices. In subsequent years I would again and again come into contact with the resurrection of Russian Buddhism for example in Dharamsala with my friend Tsering from Mongolia, in St. Petersburg with Andrey Terentjev, the chairman of the Buddhist Society in Russia, and in Moscow with Tatjana Metaxa, the deputy director of the Museum of Far Eastern Art, as well as Mr. Ngawang Gelek and his colleagues in the office of His Holiness the Dalai Lama.

ᠮᠢᠨᠤ ᠬᠠᠮᠤᠭ ᠠᠮᠢᠲᠠᠨ ᠰᠠᠶᠢᠨ ᠰᠠᠭᠤᠬᠤ ᠶᠢ

Zirlin Dascha comes from Inner Mongolia and wrote his story in Mongolian. He has two brothers and a sister, who are already grown-up. His father is a shepherd.

Lama prays that all living beings could live well.

Zirlin Dascha, 16 years old,
Original: Mongolian
From Lavizzari-Raeuber (89)

49

DASCHA

5.3. Rikon, Switzerland

Switzerland was the first European country that received Tibetan refugees. Between 1960 and 1963 over 200 Tibetan orphan children were received by the Pestalozzi Children's Village in Trogen and by Swiss families.

After the Swiss Upper House of Parliament had decided in 1963 to offer asylum initially to 1,000 Tibetan refugees from the Indian reception camps, they were settled under the care of the Swiss Red Cross in lower alpine country regions and there they were employed in local business. Today about 2,250 Tibetan refugees live in Switzerland. Up to now Tibetan settlement has been concentrated in the east of Switzerland. The village of Rikon in the Tosstal, to which I made two trips, is also situated near Zurich.

The Tibet Institute

The Tibet Institute and monastery, which was the object of my first visit to Switzerland, lies in an isolated forest location. The Institute is a foundation devoted to the cultural and spiritual care of the exiled Tibetans in Switzerland and to maintaining and preserving the Tibetan culture for coming generations of Tibetans[30]. It helps to promote cultural exchange between East and West.

In the 1960s Rikon was the place where the brothers Henri and Jacques Kuhn gave accommodation to Tibetan refugees and employed them in the Heinrich Kuhn metal goods factory. In order to ease the experience of adapting to a completely alien culture for the families who had lost their native land, the brothers Kuhn placed particular emphasis on their spiritual care. His Holiness the Dalai Lama was inspired by these ideas and sent an abbot and five monks to Rikon. As their work for the rapidly growing Tibetan community in Switzerland was proving very beneficial, the brothers Kuhn, together with a group of friends, decided to found a Tibetan Buddhist monastery, which opened in 1967. Over thirty years have passed since then, and the Tibet Institute has become an essential part of the cultural and religious life of the Tibetan community.
I had a chance to discuss this with Roswitha Reinhard, the librarian, and with one of the Kuhn brothers.

Except for the Library of Tibetan Works and Archives in Dharamsala, this library contains one of the most extensive Tibetan collections. Roswitha Reinhard helped me to enlarge my collection of stimuli to free writing and creation with some Tibetan works of art.
My contact with the Tibetan children in Rikon helped me a lot. I was able to

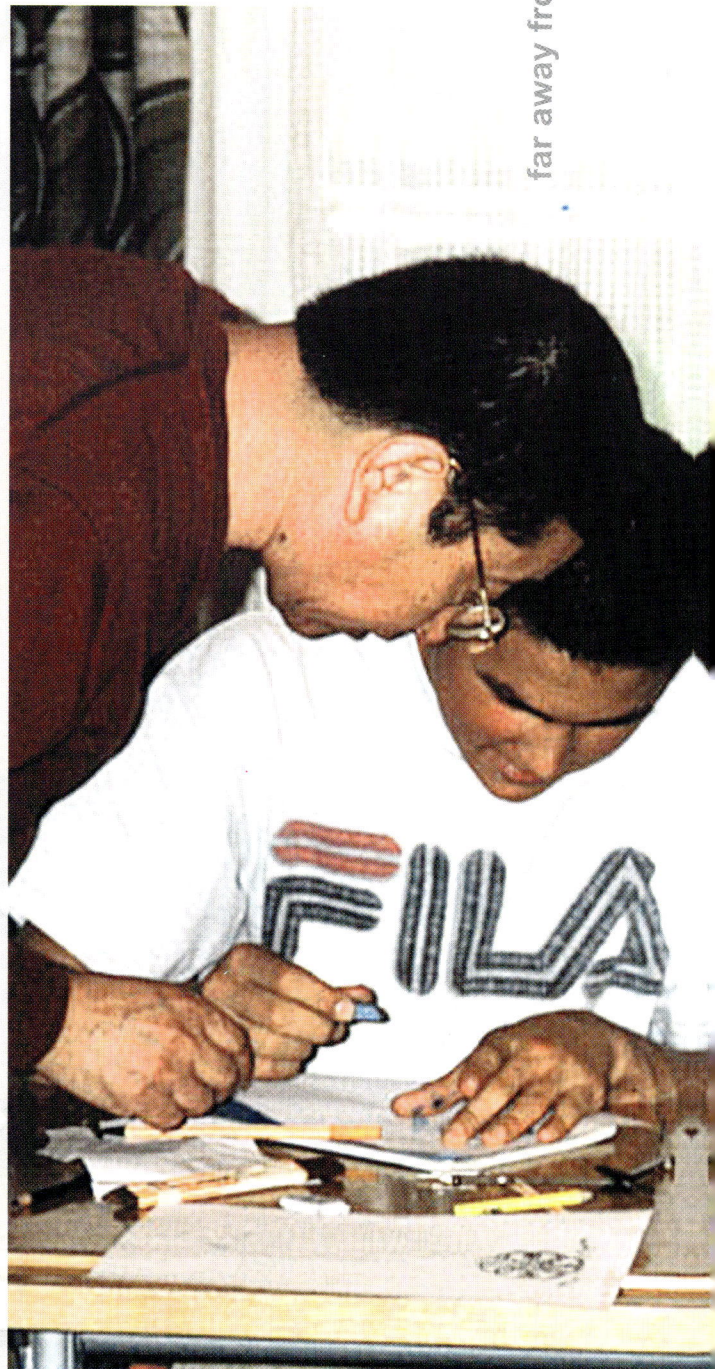

[30] See: www.tibet-institut.ch/institut.htm

sit with the children during a Tibetan lesson, given by Lama Tenzin, a monk of the Tibet Institute, and Geshe Khedup helped me to contact a Tibetan family.

Works created during Tibetan lessons

Before turning to the biographical backgrounds of these children and the works they created, I would first like to present some works which emerged during the supplementary mother-tongue lessons given by Lama Tenzin. These lessons took place in an old community centre in the village, which today also houses an inn called the Red Lion.

In one of the side rooms there are some tables and benches and a chalk board fixed to the wall. The Tibetan pupils learn their mother tongue in this classroom for an hour and a half in the afternoon. The class I attended there was for 14-17-year-olds.

The atmosphere was very relaxed, with a lot of giggling and whispering and Lama Tenzin had to make an effort to create the necessary respectful quietness. First the children practised the Tibetan characters (I drew some characters with ink as well). At intervals I talked a little bit with the mother of Tashi Kyba, who had painted the first picture. Her son had grown up in Canada and had not been here for very long.

51

LAMA TENZIN AND HIS TWO PUPILS AT A TIBETAN LESSON

SWITZERLAND

T A S H I

52

K Y I B A

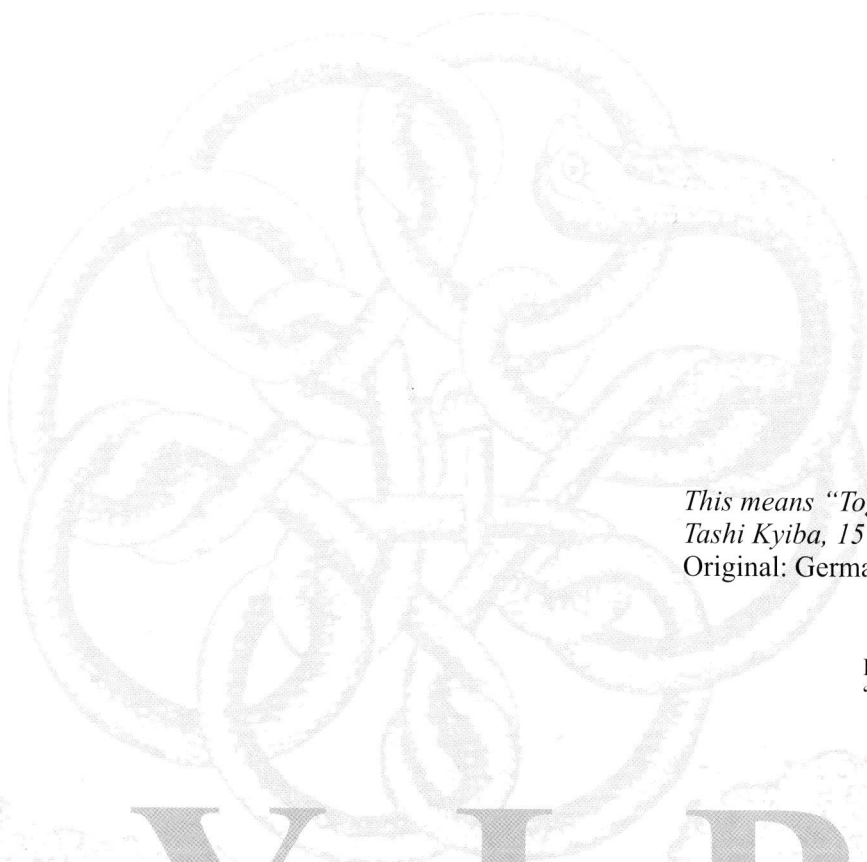

This means "Togetherness of living beings"
Tashi Kyiba, 15 years old
Original: German / Tibetan

From: Yeshi Kim, Losel
"Alternative forms of Tibetan art"

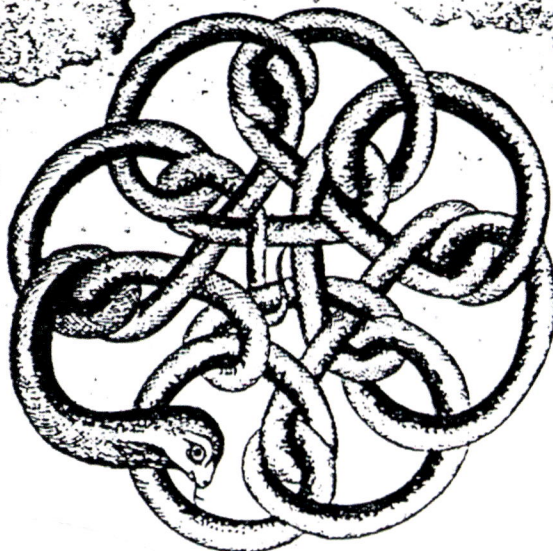

19.3.1999
Tashi.kyjba
བཀྲ་ཤིས་

 བོད་

ཕྲུག་ཆས་

53

From a Tibetan child

Das Bedeutet Zusammenhaltung von Wessen.

An interesting feature of Tenkyi's work, showing how she combines Buddhist and Christian motifs, is the angel - a figure that does not appear in Buddhism!

54

This is the angel who protects me and always takes care of me.
Tenkyi Deshar, 15 years old
Original: German / Tibetan

From: "Flying Buddha", ibid.

DESHAR

Das ist ein Engel der mich beschützt und immer auf mich aufpasst,

Tenkyi Deshar
My warm greetings

Name : Tenbyi Deshar
Alter : 15 Jahre
Datum : 19.3.99

ཨ་ནི་ཀྱི་ བཀྲ་ཤིས།
ཨ་ཤི་བལ་བོ་ལགས་སུ་ཟླ།

Three paintings and stories by Sonam (10 years old)[31]

Sonam lives together with his mother, brother and stepfather in accommodation provided by a big local firm for its employees. His mother (by then living without a husband) left Tibet with both of her children four years ago. After their escape over the Himalayas they were temporarily separated. Sonam's mother flew directly from Nepal to her sister in Rikon (her sister had come here earlier by the same route via Nepal to Switzerland), while her children went to Dharamsala to live in the TCV for two years. She took this decision in order to prepare everything for the arrival of her children in Switzerland, knowing that the TCV was a good place for them. During these first two years in Switzerland she married a Tibetan refugee who was resident there. Then she brought the children over from Dharamsala.

At present his mother works in an old people's home in the morning, coming home at lunchtime to feed her children. After this she goes on working till the evening. When I visited this place in 1999 Sonam and his brother were attending a preparatory class in a Swiss state school, where special attention was given to improving his competence in the German language.

Sonam's three pictures and stories developed at intervals of three months.

56

Sonam's first story

This is a yak!

Sonam first elaborates the figure in the set picture. Beside it he paints an apple-tree and then a big animal with horns. Round it he puts a fence. To my question whether this is a Swiss cow, he answers with indignation: *No, this is a yak like we have in Tibet!*

On the left underneath it there is a cat with a seemingly horrified or frightened expression of its face, with the hair standing on end. It seems to be fleeing from the picture. Underneath it on the right, also behind the fence, a small friendly looking yak turns up, holding the signboard *Baby*. Finally Sonam draws a man with folded arms and an enigmatic expression, standing between two yaks.

DER JAK   TIBET

DER BAUER GIBT HEU FÜR JAK. EIN MAN NIMT DEN APFEL. DIE KATZE HAT SEHR ANGST VON JAK. DAS BEBI VON JAK WEINT. ER WILL MIT DIE MUTTER BLEIBEN.
DAS BEBI DARF NICHT MIT MUTTER BLEIBEN. DER BAUER MEINT DAS BEBI gehört nicht von den Mutter und er meint Die Mutter bringt ihm uhim

[31] In this case the name is replaced by a pseudonym for personal reasons.

Sonam wrote the following text to his picture:

The yak

The farmer gives hay to the yak.
The man takes an apple.
The cat is afraid of the yak.
The yak's baby is crying.
It wants to stay with its mother.
The baby must not stay with its mother.
The farmer thinks it's not the mother's baby,
and he thinks the mother might kill it.

Sonam, 9 years old
Original: German

If one tries to interpret Sonam's picture as an analogy to his life story, it becomes evident that the separation from his mother and the loss of his native land was a traumatic experience for a child who was then only six years old. In his story he is perhaps trying to come to terms with the experience. The child's inner confusion is reflected in the picture and in the story and comes across particularly strongly in theme of the mother and baby.

57

The yak
Sonam, 9 years old
From: *Schlumpermännchen,*
from the Hamburg artists' group *Die Schlumper*

Sonam's second story

Once there was a man and a yak.
The man and the yak think that the river is very beautiful.
Both have also a fir-tree and a house[32].

Sonam, 9 years old
Original: German

Sonam sends this story to me on his own initiative (by post for Christmas). Again he takes up the yak theme, which is apparently an important feature of his native land for him. In addition there is a symbol from his new surroundings: a Christmas tree! Possibly the house that is painted beside it can be interpreted as a sign of his psychological anchoring in the new surroundings. The individual elements are relatively unconnected with each other. He has written the story on a slip of paper and then stuck it to the picture with a piece of sellotape.

Sonam's third story

Here God is flying
A nice cloud appears now.
Then a man comes:
"Here God is flying!"

Then comes a child and asks:
"May I stand on your head, so that I can see God?"
Then comes another child and pulls his coat.
But the man always looks up because God is more important.

Actually we must point at God with a hand,
Not with the finger!
This is not good!
A man is not good because he points with a finger.

Sonam, 10 years old
Original: German

It is clear that Sonam has learned a lot since he painted the first picture half a year earlier. Now he can already express complex thoughts in a foreign language well. His handwriting and painting skills have also developed.

58

In terms of content, the picture subtly represents the relationships of various people to each other as well as their relation to God (Sonam does not speak about Buddha). In the last sentence of his story, backed by the moral authority of his religion, he criticises one of the people.

One may presume that Sonam identifies himself with the child who is depicted as being barred from seeing God by the man in the coat. The child asks the man for help, but the man is too preoccupied with his own pious thoughts to notice the child. Sonam accepts the higher order of events (because God is more important). However, he criticises the mistaken behaviour of the man (pointing at God with a finger), comparing it with the correct gesture according to Buddhist teaching (always to point at a person with the whole hand). This behavioural rule is found in the Tibetan Buddhist tradition as early as the 8th century AD in a text by the famous Buddhist scholar Santideva:

> *He may not give orders with a finger,*
> *but politely with the whole right hand.*
> *Similarly he shows the way as well[33].*

Generally this work shows that Sonam is on the way to re-gaining his identity. Now he knows how to stand up for his own point of view in a critical situation, and he is no longer helpless in reacting to the behaviour of others (like the baby in his first story). From his own cultural and religious roots he is able to derive a belief structure that helps him to solve his problems.

59

Jetzt kommt so schöre wolke dan kommt ein Mann

und er schaut nach oben dan kammt ein Goot dan ruft der Mann hier fliegt ein Goot deu kommt ein Kind und fragt darf ich auf deine kopf stehen das ich Goot sehen kann er sagt ja, ein andere Kind fragte darf ich auf deine kopf stehen damit ich goot sehen kann er sagte ja. Dan kommt ein andere Kind zieht sein Mantel der Mann schaut immer oben weil goot wichtiger iste. Eingtlich mösen wier mit

[33] See Santideva "Eintritt in das Leben zur Erleuchtung", Muenchen 1981, p.60 (ch.5,vers 94)

Here God is flying
Sonam, 10 years old

From: "Flying Buddha",
from Losel "Alternative forms of Tibetan art", Dharamsala, n.d.

5.4. Hamburg, Germany

Only a few Tibetans (altogether about 10 to 15) live in Hamburg. "Tibet" is the name of one cosy restaurant in Hamburg-Altona, which is run by a Tibetan family. There are two sons in this family. Phurbu, the mother, a friendly person who is actively engaged in Tibetan issues, is immediately prepared to take part in my project. She promises to talk with her sons and invites me to a common "session" in her flat which is situated in the house next to the restaurant. The decor of the flat is a mixture of traditional Tibetan and modern western. Both brothers are already waiting for me and playing with their cats. After my explanations they eagerly get down to work at the table in the living room.

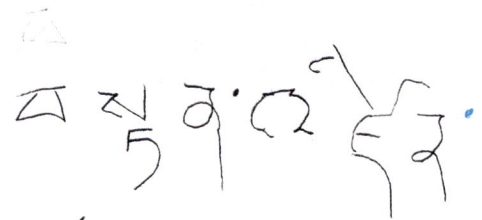

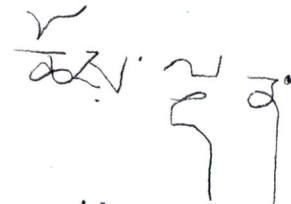

    While eight-year-old Tenjing Choenden is painting his picture he gets up constantly, runs into the corridor and soon comes back to paint further. When I spoke to him about this he said: "We have a picture of the Potala[34] in Lhasa in the corridor. I always count how many windows there are in the Potala because I would like to paint the same in my picture!"

    Tenjing writes in German, adding his name carefully and with great effort in Tibetan characters, which his mother taught him. I am a little astonished to learn that at school he is known only under the name "Sven". His mother thinks that this name is more easily accepted at school.

60

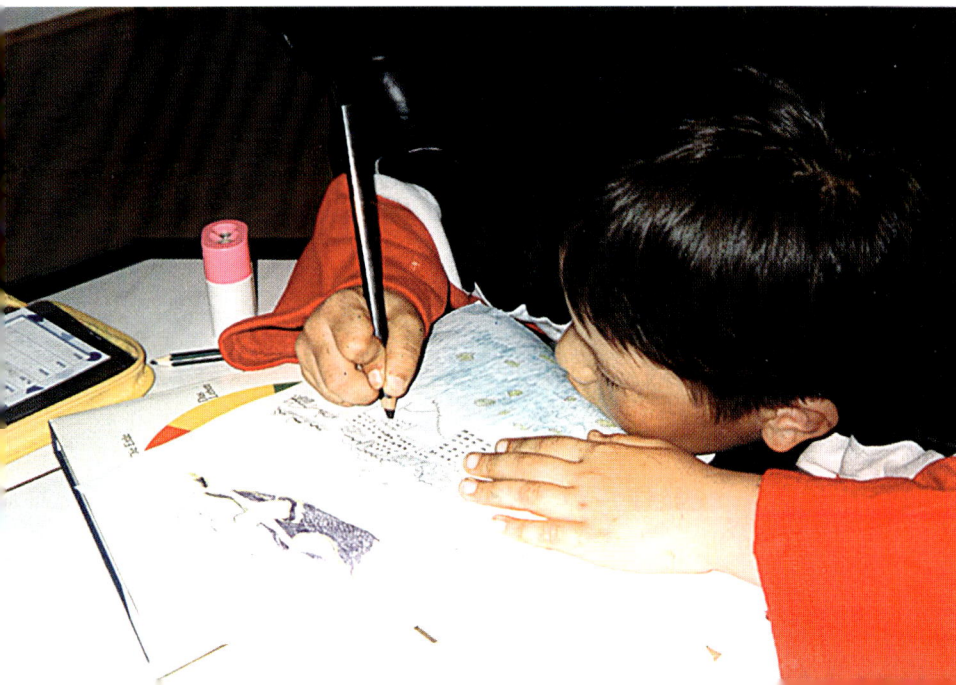

[34] *Potala Palace*: Winter Palace of the Dalai Lamas since the great Fifth Dalai Lama situated above the Lhasa valley, Tibet (UNESCO World Heritage Site)

das ist Tibet

Man on a flying carpet
This man on the flying carpet is a Tibetan monk, who is flying over Tibet, where the Potala is and where the Tibetan Snow Mountains are.

Dalai Lama is looking through the window and admiring Tibet.

Tenjing, 8 years old
Original: German

"This is Tibet"
Man on a flying carpet
Tenjing, 8 years old

From: "Flying Buddha",
from Losel "Alternative forms
of Tibetan art", Dharamsala, n.d.

5.5. LEH, LADAKH

Audience with His Holiness the 14th Dalai Lama in Leh, 27 May 1999

The main reason of my trip to Ladakh was the audience with His Holiness the 14th Dalai Lama. This audience had been prepared long in advance. Dr. Paul Belanger, Director of UNESCO Institute for Education in Hamburg at that time wrote a recommendation letter for me which was answered promptly by the Office of His Holiness in Dharamsala. The preparatory work was then continued by e-mail (a form of communication which was still a novelty for my institute in Hamburg but already common practice in India). At first the audience was planned to take place in Dharamsala, but a few weeks before the appointment I received a message that it would take place in Ladakh, as His Holiness the Dalai Lama would be holding teaching sessions there. In great haste I was able to re-book my trip. Unfortunately Valerii told me two days before departure that he had to drop out (important business in Russian that could not be postponed). At Delhi airport Sonam Wangchuk (my contact person in Nepal) was waiting for me. To pass the time before my connecting flight to Ladakh he took me to Majnu-Katilla, a Tibetan refugee centre on the outskirts of Delhi.

Back at the airport there was uncertainty about whether the fine weather would last long enough to get to Ladakh by plane (the planes to Leh take off only in fine weather and are scheduled to fly only every few days). Luck was with me, and I found myself *en route* to Leh, looking out at a fantastic view of the Himalayas.

In my hotel in Leh, the only guests besides me were one Japanese lady and two Americans from Seattle who were doing teacher training at the local TCV. Tenzin Takla, who was coordinating the trip to Ladakh for the Dalai Lama, called me considerately immediately after my arrival. We fixed a meeting with Venerable Lhakdor, the personal interpreter of His Holiness, so that I could discuss with him my questions for the audience. The next morning I woke up with a horrible headache and felt quite weak. After all, Leh is situated at a height of at least 3,500 metres. A few hours later I felt better after drinking many cups of strong coffee.

My stay was divided between the work in the TCV at Ladakh (see below) and the teaching sessions of the Dalai Lama, which took place in a big open meadow. Ladakhis, Tibetans and other mountain folk had arrived from the most remote valleys, and it was fantastic to see them in their colourful national costumes. I was allowed to sit at the front beside the monks with a little group of foreigners.

Of course my whole 10-days was dominated by the question: "When will the audience take place?" The weather was unusual. There was a great deal of rain and some of the teaching sessions had to be postponed, because the people could not sit for hours in the puddles which had appeared in the meadow. This again caused changes in the timetable. Moreover, a few days later military planes were permanently thundering across the sky above our heads, a new episode in the conflict between India and Pakistan, which one could feel at close quarters in Ladakh.

Finally, on the second last day of my stay, I got the message that the audience could take place at lunch time the following day! Yoshi Fredisdorf, the Japanese lady from my hotel, accompanied me and took photos. Carrying pictures and stories of many Tibetan children, I headed punctually for the residence of the Dalai Lama, which is situated outside Leh, close to the place where the teachings take place. The teachings were already over and some 30,000 people were flooding along what appeared to be the only street in the direction of Leh. There was no way to get through the crowd, and I started panicking lest I should miss my audience.

But the taxi driver was resourceful and managed to drive his jeep along bumpy "secret" tracks in the direction of the residence. Almost on time I came to the gate where I was already awaited. Yoshi and I were thoroughly checked (security precautions are very strict), and finally we were guided into the audience room. Near the sitting area there was a high throne. The Dalai Lama and his entourage came in almost silently. I had written down everything that I most wanted to say, but now I was feeling rather nervous. Soon this tension dissolved when I showed His Holiness the pictures and stories of the Tibetan children, which he examined attentively and with great empathy. His Holiness laughed heartily over some of the works, others made him sad and thoughtful. After that I was in my element and was able to engage in a dialogue with him arising from the children's works about education in exile, about the importance of creativity, about imparting Tibetan culture and tradition while taking account of more "modern" elements.

His Holiness was especially taken with one of the works of art which the children were given as a starting point for their pictures and stories, namely from Valery Bugrov's land art project *Heaven and Earth*. This is a large circular mirror (about 180 square metres), installed in a field in Luneburg Heath in northern Germany[35], which reflects the sky, the sun, moon, stars and clouds, presenting a constantly changing spectacle according to season, time of day and different weather conditions.

At the end of the audience - probably inspired by this work - His Holiness took my pen and wrote a poem of his own. Everyone present fell silent, as this was undoubtedly a very unusual event. When he had finished the poem he recited it in a sonorous voice in Tibetan, after which it was translated into English by Venerable Lhakdor[36].

[35]Cf. Fig. On the cover page
[36]Cf. introduction

During the audience

Situation of the Tibetan refugees in Ladakh[37]

About 6,500 Tibetan refugees live in Ladakh, a region on the border of North-West India and Tibet. Approximately 4,000 settled Tibetans are divided among eleven centres, of which Choklamsar is the biggest. In addition there are about 2,500 Tibetan nomads and semi-nomads, who roam around the Changtang Highlands near the Tibetan border. The settlements in Ladakh are among the most remote and the least developed of the Tibetan exile communities today.

The Tibetan refugee centre Sonamling in Choklamsar lies nine kilometres south of Leh. The centre was built in the 1970s in order to provide accommodation for Tibetan refugees, most of whom had fled from the Changtang plateau to India in 1961-64. The refugee centre lies at a height of 3,500 metres in a sandy desert. Newcomers are provided by the Indian government with a piece of land where they can grow grain and vegetables. Many Tibetans work in the Indian army or in road-building. Thirty years after their escape the Tibetans in exile are still dependent on regular support from international assistance funds and the government.

64   *The children in a classroom in the TCV Ladakh in Choklamsar*

[37] Cf. in the following: Mattausch, Jutta "Ladakh und Zanskar", Bielefeld 1996, p. 266-269

In 1975 the Tibetan Children's Village was founded in Choklamsar with the help of international donations (mainly from the Hermann Gmeiner Fund). Besides the Children's' Village school and the one in Choklamsar, there are seven schools further away to which the children are ferried. The schools offer education up to secondary level. At present there more than 1,600 children living in the village, mostly orphans. The TCV has its own kindergarten as a school for the primary and middle levels up to the 10th grade. By now seven other schools have been founded in the area around the TCV as well as the centre for hand crafts, a school for vocational training and an old people's home.

65

Children in the TCV Ladakh in Choklamsar at work

Tenzin was born in the refugee centre and lives there together with his parents, grandparents and sister. His father is a teacher in the TCV. Tenzin says that he likes living in the refugee centre and besides his family he has many friends there. Later he would like to become an artist. His teacher says that he is a good pupil. His hobby is playing football.

Two works by Tenzin, which he created in the course of a day, exemplify different themes that play an important role in his life[38]. While in his first story he speaks about something very typical for Tibet (namely a yak), his second work deals with a more "transcultural" phenomenon which fascinates him and which he knows from the mass media, namely an international football match broadcast on TV.

66 **The name of this beautiful and helpful creature is "Yak".**
This is a creature which can only be seen in our country Tibet.
It lives in the cooler areas.
It is useful for us, as it gives us milk to drink and by its wool we can make sweaters.
So the name of this beautiful and helpful creature is "Yak".

Tenzin, 8 years old, a boy, TCV Ladakh
Original: English

Tenzin's picture radiates cheerfulness and harmony. The main figure, a shaggy Tibetan yak, is depicted in surroundings that are typical for his homeland. In the background one can see the snow-covered Himalayas and the Tibetan prayer flags fluttering above the peaks. The yak is standing in a lush green meadow through which a river is winding. A Buddhist oratory is also situated there (on the right).

Tenzin describes the valuable abilities of the yak objectively and precisely. On the emotional level one can observe Tenzin's pride in the yak, which is so important for his culture.

The name of this beautiful and helpful creature is "Yak"
Tenzin, 8 years old

From: Bull's Head by Pablo Picasso.

This is a creature which can only seen in our country Tibet. It live in the cooler areas. As its also is useful to us. As it gives us milk to drink and by its wool we can make swater. So the name of this beautiful and helpfull creature is "Yak"

[38] *A note about the children's painting technique in the TCV, Ladakh*: In contrast to the Tibetan children in Switzerland and Nepal, those in the TCV in Ladakh did not integrate the set picture into their own works, but rather re-created it in their own way and then put it into a context imagined by themselves. This is probably because in their art lessons at school they are used to drawing set objects and pictures.

Match between Argentina and Brazil
This is the match between Argentina and Brazil.
Argentina lost the match after the goal which was shot by Ronaldo.
The goalkeeper Roa missed the ball.
The best player of the match is Ronaldo, the number nine of the Brazilian team.

Tenzin, 8 years old, a boy, TCV
Ladakh
Original: English

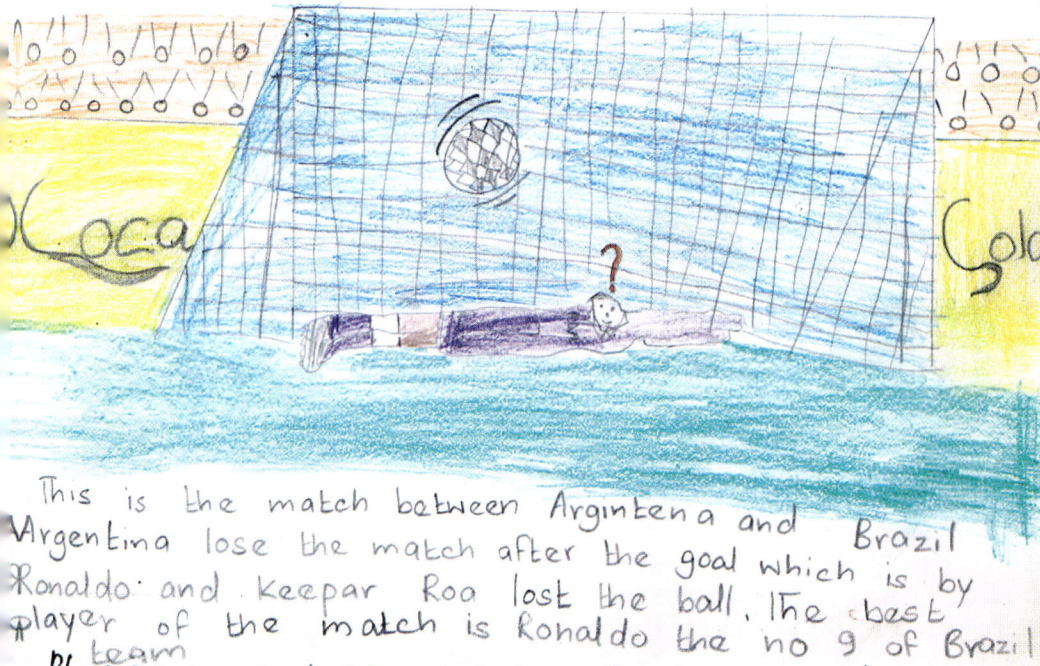

Match between Argentina and Brazil
Tenzin, 8 years old

From: *Treppensteiger (stair climbers)*
by the Hamburg artists' group *Die Schlumper*

Tenzin's second painting and story are linked with his personal hobby playing football. He presents the theme in a humorous way. In the centre there a confused looking goalkeeper, who is lying on the ground in front of his goal. A question mark hovers symbolically over his head while the football moves towards the goal at high speed. The goal is framed by the well-known logo for Coca-Cola, a typical Western consumer product.

In his story he writes about an international football match, mentioning two leading players that he has heard about. The topic of football plays an important role in many pictures and stories of the Tibetan children.

It is astonishing that the eight-year-old Tenzin, like many other Tibetan children, can already write his fantasy stories in English without help. No one told him to write in English, but he did so on his own initiative.

5.6. Dharamsala, India

Dharamsala has been the home of His Holiness the Dalai Lama and Headquarters of his Government in Exile since 1960. It is situated in Himachal Pradesh, northern India. This town with 17,000 inhabitants is divided into many separate districts. It is built close to the snow line and stretches along a ridge of the Dhauladar range. Within the town, the height above sea level varies greatly. Lower Dharamsala, an Indian mountain village, lies at a height of 1,250 metres. Higher up is Ganchen Kyishong, where the Tibetan government in exile has its headquarters. Further up, at 2,000 metres, is the district of McLeod Ganj. The Tibetan Children's village is higher still.

In McLeod Ganj is the Namgyal monastery, with the residence of His Holiness the Dalai Lama and the Tibetan settlement. There are also many hotels, restaurants and shops, which are mainly run by Tibetans. In this place one can meet a colourful mixture of people: Tibetan refugees, Buddhist nuns and monks from all over the world, Tibetans who have specially come across the Himalayas to see the Dalai Lama and then return home, researchers from many different countries, and young hippies, many of them Israelis who have just finished their military service.

The plan for me to go to Dharamsala arose in 1999 after a conversation with Ngawang Gelek, a representative of Dalai Lama who was at that time in Moscow. He helped me to prepare everything necessary for the trip. I first went to this very special place in the summer 2000 (ignoring Ngawang Gelek's advice to avoid the monsoon season!) with my then 18-year-old son Maxim. At the airport in Delhi we were met by two Tibetans and then went in a jeep further to the north. After heavy rain and 12-hour drive we arrived at midnight and checked into the Tibet hotel.

One day, while attending the public Buddhist seminars in the library, located in the Ganchen Kyishong district, I became acquainted with Tsering, a Mongolian lady, who had been deeply immersed in Buddhist studies there for many years and before that had studied fine arts in Moscow. In subsequent years she became one of my main contact persons. Thanks to her I met Rinchen Khandro Choegyal, the former Minister for Education and director of the Tibetan Nuns Project, as well as ("Nechung Oracle"), Medium of the State Oracle of His Holiness the Dalai Lama. In 2001 the latter painted a picture for my project.

68

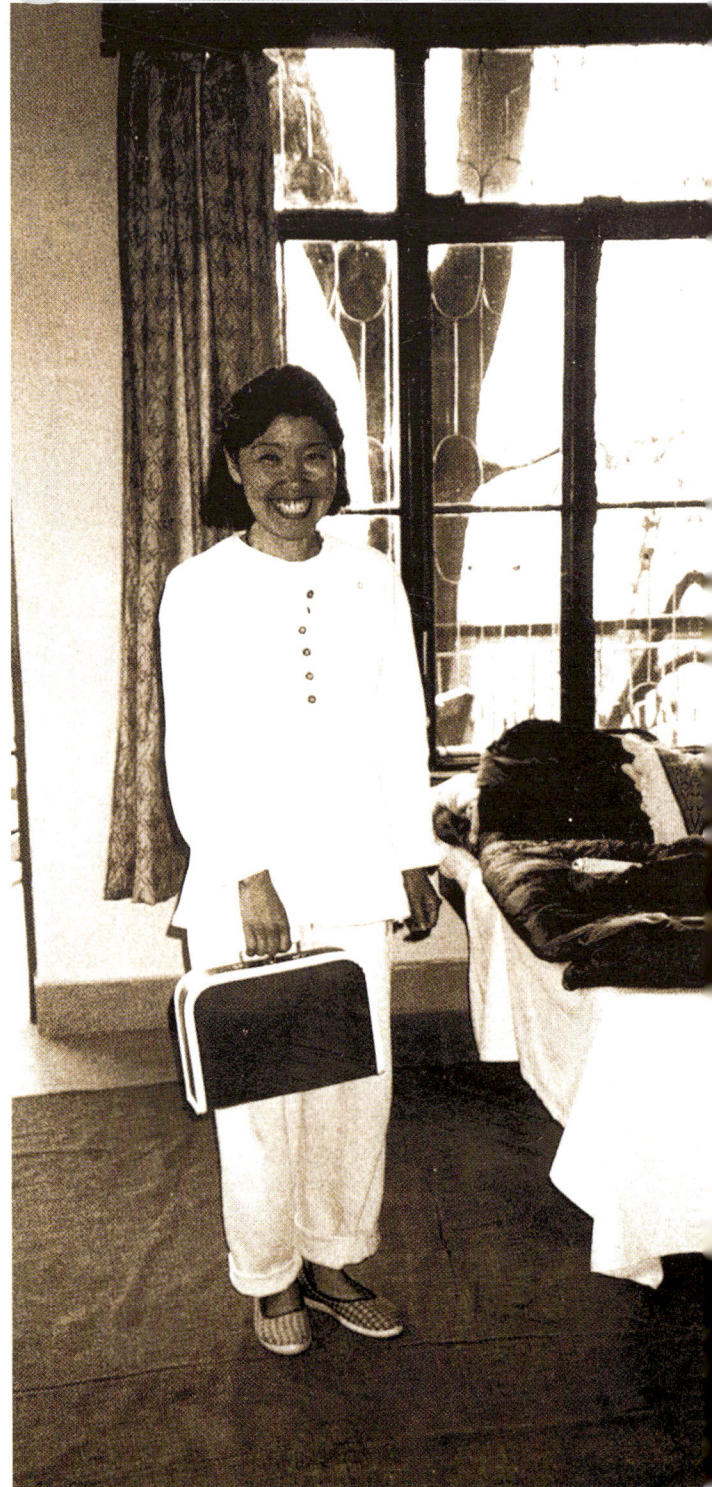

Tsering (in Ü-pel Guesthouse, Ganchen Kyishong)

Children in the Upper-TCV, Dharamsala

Working with the children in the TCV, Upper Dharamsala

This TCV is the biggest and serves as a model for all the Tibetan Children's Villages. It has 41 communities, resembling extended families, as well as hostels for older children, an infants' home, a hospital and a school with four different levels, namely for very young children, older children, adolescents and young people. At present there are more than 2,300 children in the TCV. The central office for all Tibetan Children's Villages, headed by Jetsun Pema, is also located there.

TCV-children and Mr. Phuntsok Tsering (headmaster elementary school)

In the following pages I present a variety of children's pictures and stories as well as extracts from interviews with children with various different types of experience behind them, who live and go to school in the TCV Dharamsala. I visited these children every year over a period of four years (1999-2003). Each year, when I met them again, I had the opportunity to work with them in their writing and painting, and of course to speak with them. Each time I brought different writing stimuli with me. At first I worked mainly with works of art from all over the world, but later on poems played an increasing role.

69

I N D I A

TENZIN TSANGYANG, TENZIN SAMTEN, RINCHEN WANGMO AND JAMYANG BOKTO: glimpses into their lives (their languages, their wishes and hopes)

Here I would like to introduce four children with whom I had close contact over this whole period. For example, when I met Tenzin Tsangyang in 2000, she was 11 years old. When I went to see her in 2003 she was already an adolescent girl of 14 years old. Over that period it was interesting for me to share in her inner development and observe how it was reflected in her works.

The statements and stories of the four children, which are presented largely without commentary, spotlight certain essential aspects of their lives and circumstances as Tibetan refugees in exile. They deal selectively with such areas as their families, wishes, fears and hopes for the future as well as with language issues.

The "core group" of children with whom I worked intensively over the years included also Tenzin Tsokij and Ngawang Migmar, both of whom are represented in the second part of this book through their pictures and writings, especially in the section devoted to poems (6.6).

4 LANGUAGE PORTRAITS: TENZIN TSANGJANG, TENZIN SAMTEN, RINCHEN WANGMO, JAMJANG BOKTO

My languages

In order to enable the children to express on the emotional level their feelings about the important issue of language, a method was used involving the concept of "language portraits"[40].

Working with language portraits[41]

To create their language portraits the children are given an outline of a human figure, in which they can paint visual impressions of their languages with crayons. They have absolute freedom of expression, i.e. they can use their imaginations and paint their images all within the figure or in some parts of it. They can also add clothes, paint hair on the head or put "language shoes" on the feet. As these four examples show, the children have different ideas about how their languages should be located in various parts of the body. They are not told how they should do this, nor whether they should add any comments orally or in writing. Furthermore nothing is said to them about how well one needs to know a language in order to "paint" it. This should be left as open as possible when they are given the task, so as to include "all languages that you know or can speak a little bit". It is important that the children express their own thoughts about their languages and are not inhibited by preconceived expectations.

I decided to extend their task by asking them to add an example of one word from every language they had heard. This brought some humorous results (e.g. Rinchen Wangmo's words in German!).

Tenzin Tsangjang's language portrait
Tibetan:
Tenzin has filled in her outline figure with miniature drawings.
Her mother tongue, Tibetan, is in the centre of the figure. The outline of Tibet fills the entire torso, which contains plants and animals typical of Tibet.

Tenzin has written the commentary:
Tibetan is my mother tongue. I have drawn an outline map of Tibet and I have also drawn the environment of Tibet before the invasion of the Chinese.

[40] Krumm, Hans-Jurgen, *Kinder und ihre Sprachen lebendige Mehrsprachigkeit* (Wien, Eviva-Verlag, 2001).
[41] Cf. Krumm, Hans-Jurgen "Mein Bauch ist italienisch..." In: Grundschule: Sprachen 7/2002, pp. 37ff.

English is shown in the head of the figure.
I drew the flag of the USA. And I drew some industries as this country is full of industries and is also a fully developed country.

Hindi (arms) and **Nepalese** (legs) are also given comments by Tenzin relating to the level of the development of these countries.

About Hindi:
I drew some fields, as in India more than 80% of the population are farmers. But the country is now becoming a developed country.

About Nepalese:
I speak English with my mother and father about my school subjects. I speak Hindi with the people who are Indians, and I speak Nepali with my cousins in Kathmandu. At school I speak mostly Tibetan.

Tenzin Samten language portrait.
Tenzin Samten speaks fluent Tibetan and English, also a little Nepali and Hindi and some words in Spanish ("Mexican"). Tibetan is central for him and emotionally very important (it is placed in the heart area). English is more cognitively controlled (he puts it in the head). Nepali and Hindi are given a rather peripheral position in the right leg, and finally some pieces of Spanish can be found in the left foot.

Rinchen Wangmo's language portrait.
Rinchen Wangmo places Tibetan and English, both of which she knows well, close to each other in the heart area, while Hindi belongs more to the head. Her attempt to speak a little bit of German is touching (it is placed in a big toe!):

> *"A ve thesan"* - "Auf Wiedersehen" (Bye-bye)
> *"Go din a ben"* - "Guten Abend" (Good evening)
> *"Go din morgan"* - "Guten Morgen" (Good morning)

Jamyang Bokto's language portrait.
Jamyang Bokto places his languages artistically in the figure. The Tibetan flag, delicately traced out, is given a central position in the upper part of the torso and is surrounded with a halo, as shown in figures of Buddha. He puts more flags, almost like chakras, along the spine (Korean, Japanese, Indian, English), symbolising the languages spoken by him. Finally he adds Chinese in the left leg and Pakistani in the right leg.

It emerged in the conversation that Jamyang Bokto has a real talent for languages. He is fluent in Korean and Tibetan (his mother tongues) and has very good English. In addition he knows some Japanese, Hindi, Pakistani and Chinese, and says that he can also write them a little bit. This is how he describes his everyday use of his languages:

I speak English, Tibetan, Hindi, and Korean
In my family we speak mostly Korean (at home).
When I speak with Indian, I speak Hindi.
At school I speak Tibetan and English with my teachers and friends.

71

My name: Tenzin Tsangyang
My languages: Tibetan, English, Nepali, Hindi

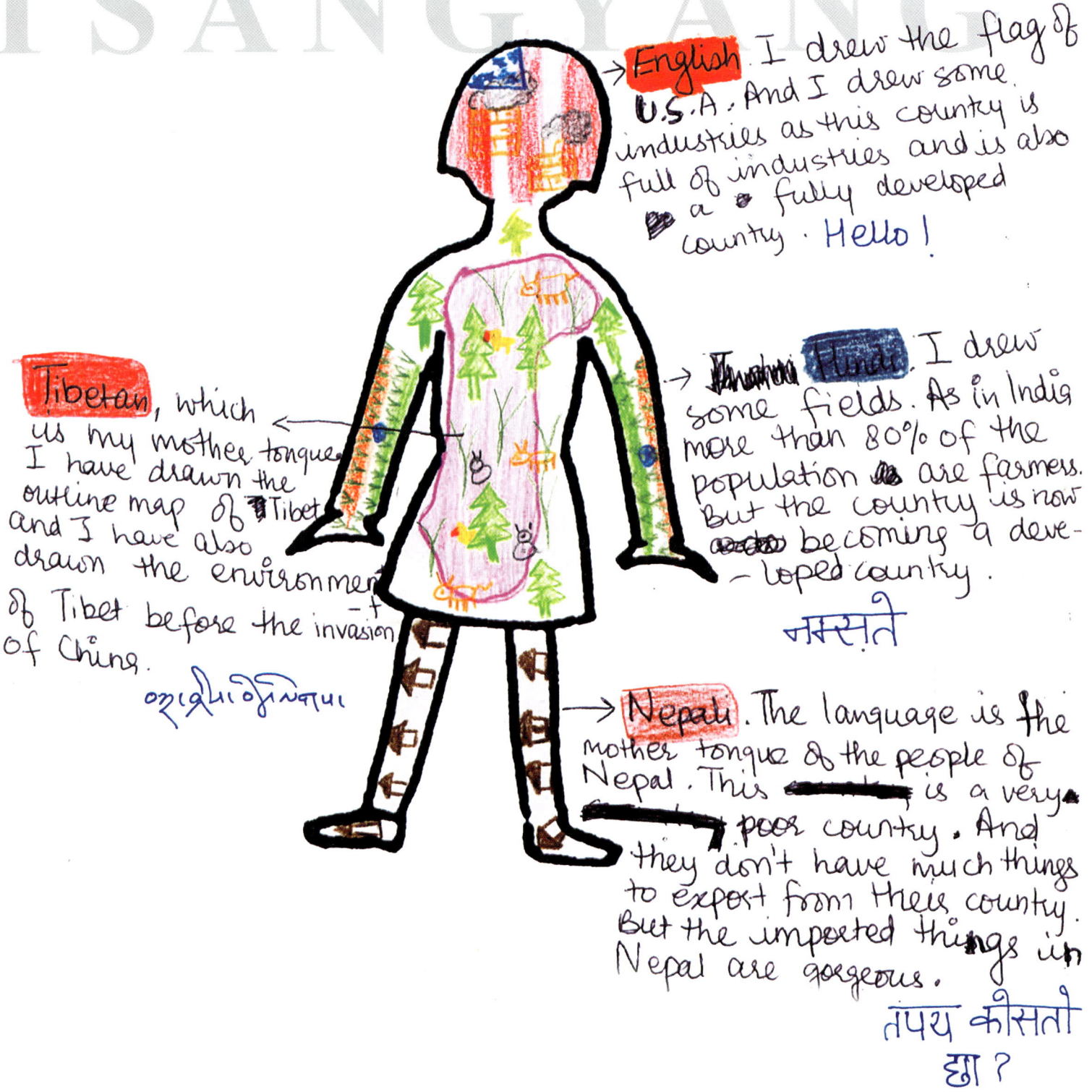

English. I drew the flag of U.S.A. And I drew some industries as this country is full of industries and is also a fully developed country. Hello!

Tibetan, which us my mother tongue. I have drawn the outline map of Tibet and I have also drawn the environment of Tibet before the invasion of China.

ཀ་ར་ཤྲི་བོ་གུ་ཐལ་པ།

Hindi. I drew some fields. As in India more than 80% of the population are farmers. But the country is now becoming a developed country.

नमस्ते

Nepali. The language is the mother tongue of the people of Nepal. This is a very poor country. And they don't have much things to export from their country. But the imported things in Nepal are gorgeous.

तपय कीसतो छा ?

My name: Tenzin Samten
My languages: Tibetan, Hindi, English, Mexican

NEPAL

English: Bye Bye my friend

धारम से जोरे
वा उल

Nepal
रमारी जानुस
हेला साथी

Tibetan
गाणब्बाप्पु
ष्ण्णप

Mexican
astalavista
Amega

T E N Z I N
S A M T E N

Tibetan

འཇུ་ཡང་བོག་ཏོ་~ (Taohi Belek)

My name: Jamyang Bokto
My languages: Tibetan,

Korea
Yoboseho ~ (Hello)

India
नास्साती ~ (Hello)

Chiness
Woo i ne,
(I love you)

Japan
(Onhneche wa

England
(How do yo do?

Pakistan
Maleek ho salam

Lam fine,

JAMYANG
BOKTO

Friendship forever

I want to make friendship forever with other
countries.
When I get my country's freedom, I will need
help from other countries.
We don't have many people
and I will need the support of other countries.

Tenzin Tsangyang, 11 years old
Original: English

76

Friendship forever
Tenzin Tsangyang, 11 years old

From a Siberian cave painting

Name: Tenzin Tsangyang
age: 11
address: upper T.C.V.
nationality: Tibetan
(Girl)

Nomads

In Tibet most of the people are nomads.
They keep changing home from place to place.
They keep yaks, sheep and sheepdogs as their pets.
They also have farms.
Nomads live in grass land.
They live in tents.

Tenzin Tsangyang, 11 years old
Original: English

Nomads
Tenzin Tsangyang, 11 years old

Made from the set picture with coloured paper, cut up and stuck on with paste.

TSANGYANG

Tenzin Tsangyang, a girl

Tenzin Tsangyang was born in 1988 in Dharamsala, northern India[39]

My family

I have lived in the TCV since I was three years old. Then I went to Kathmandu because my parents were moved there to the Tibetan representative office. In 1999 my father was moved back to the TCV in Dharamsala, so the whole family came back here.

There are four members in my family: my father, my mother, my younger sister and myself. My father is a treasurer in a business central office and my mother is a nurse at the Ministry of Health of the government in exile. My younger sister is in the second class at the same school as me.

My biggest fear

My biggest fear starts at night.
Oh! I am really afraid of the night.
I am also afraid to go to veranda which is right outside our house.

My dream

78

One night I had a very strange dream.
I was going to the market and bought a dozen of bananas. And when I was giving money to the fruit-seller, a monkey came unexpectedly and grabbed the bananas. Suddenly I woke up. But there was nothing wrong. So I slept in again. And when I got up the next morning a monkey really came into our house and was really eating the bananas from our fruit basket.

One day I would like to be …

…a heart specialist as in the present community we, Tibetan people, often suffer from heart problems, and we don't have a good heart specialist right now in the Tibetan community. So I want to become one.

[39] The conversations selectively presented here were held mainly in March 2002 and March 2003 (in English).

The clever rabbit
Usually crocodiles are very cruel and fierce and eat whatever they get.
One day it met a rabbit.
And the rabbit was about to be eaten, Immediately the rabbit showed his long ears and said to the crocodile: "Peace!"
The rabbit gave advice to the crocodile.
And the crocodile went back into the sea as a wiser crocodile.

Tenzin Tsangyang, 12 years old
Original: English

Tenzin's story, which is reminiscent of a fable, probably refers to the Tibetan folk tale *The Clever Rabbit*[42]. The "Peace" sign is an important symbol in the Tibetan movement for freedom (*Free Tibet!*)[43].

79

Usually the crocodiles are very cruel and fierce and eat whatever he gets. And one day he met a rabbit and the rabbit was about to be eaten, immediately the rabbit showed his long ears and said "PEACE to the crocodile and the crocodile was advised by the rabbit and went back into the sea as a wiser crocodile.

The clever rabbit
Tenzin Tsangyang, 12 years old

From one of the ambiguous figures originally developed by the philosopher Ludwig Wittgenstein (1889-1951). Depending on which way one turns the figure, it looks like a crocodile or like a rabbit or something else.

[42] *The Clever Rabbit*, a Tibetan folk tale published by the Tibetan Children Villages (n.d.).
[43] For further works by Tenzin Tsangyang see the following chapter

Tenzin Samten was born in 1988 in Nepal. He has lived in the TCV for three years.

My family
I have no longer my father, only my mother is in thoughts with me to share my feelings. My father was a manager of a carpet factory. When my father died, my mother went to America to help her relatives. That's why we came here to Dharamsala for help. These days we have a normal life… I have three sisters as friends and one brother as a partner.

My biggest fear
When my mother leaves me alone and lost in this world.

Kamphel-lade

Delo she is the house wife
My Mother 45 years

Sonam Choekyi
Eldest sister
help my with my mom 33 years

My brother is Kunga
a student 20 years

Its Me student
14

Sister
Ngadon is 12
years
student

My Sister Nurse
is nurse 30 years
Chemi Kalsang

My father was a manager of a carpet factory. When my father in TCV Died my mother went to America for help with my mother relatives. Thats why we came here in Dharamsala for help. This days we stay in a normal life. When I become big I am going be do work in video game industry and fed them happily.

My family
Tenzin Samten, 14 years old

Profession
I would like to be a ~~men~~ Video game designer
Tenzin Samten   Six Dhug   7l= 18   Roll no 8443

Why? Please, explain!

I have promised my whole family that I will
fed them weel as I can so I wished to be a video game
designer. They also believed me very much so I cannot break their heart.
I choose this work because it is not so easy.

One day I would like to be …

… a video game designer.
I chose this work because it is not so easy.
I have promised to my whole family that I will feed them as well as I can.
They believe in me so much that I cannot break their hearts.

These works were done in March 2002.

81

One day I would like to be …
Tenzin Samten, 14 years old

SAMTEN

Rinchen Wangmo was born in 1989 in the Kham province of Tibet. She was brought to India by her mother in 1995.

My family

My family is in Tibet. My mother is a housewife. My father was a doctor, but he had problems with money. Now they are farmers and have lots of problems because they do not get any help and are old. My sister and little brother live in India. I try to study hard in order to support my family later. I miss my parents and love them very much. I did not know the face of my grandpa because he was killed in a Chinese revolt. Also my uncle fought with the Chinese, but he is alive. I am very proud of my grandpa and my uncle.

My biggest fear

To be alone at night and to see a cat that crosses my way.

Nightmare

I was called by someone from the spooky forest. My feet started to step towards the forest but my mind refused to go. Something terrible was about to happen. My heart started thumping so hard when a gust of wind harshly touched my skin. It was very eerie, I could not bear crying. Suddenly a very quiet voice came close. It was my mum and I was just having a nightmare.

One day I would like to be …

82 *…a great doctor. I would like to work in the Tibetan community which brought much knowledge into my dark life. I will help and serve as much as possible without getting money for this.*

I have got a lot of experience from my grandma. She had to suffer a lot and I have promised to myself to become a good doctor who can take good care of the patients and who is honest. Now my grandma died.

A bird, a monkey and a dog

A bird, a monkey and a dog were having a solemn discussion about hunters who destroyed their homes and they were planning how to punish them. The three animals made a group to help each other. They kicked all the hunters out of the forest by scaring them. But no animal killed a single hunter as they knew that was a sin.
All the animals in the forest lived happily ever after.

Rinchen Wangmo, 13 years old
Original: English

A bird, a monkey and a dog
Rinchen Wangmo, 13 years old

The stimulus comes from the collection *Children's paintings from the Ghetto Terezin*, in the archive of the Jewish Museum, Prague (I explained the origin of these pictures to the children).

J. Spiha'

83

Birds, Monkey and dog were having a solemm discussion on hunters who destroyed their homes. and planning to punish them. The three animals make big group to help them. They kick all the hunters out of the forest by makeing them scared But no animals didn't kill a single hunter as they knew the sin. All the animals in the Forest lived happily every after.

Lord Buddha came to Tibet
I imagined that after the
13th Dalai Lama had died,
Lord Buddha came to Tibet
and said that
the 14th Dalai Lama would be born
in Amdo Taktser in 1935.
He will change the world.

Jamyang Bokto, 12 years old

84

Name: Jamyang BokTo
age: 12
address: T.C.V. School
nationality: Tibetan

I imagied that after the 13th Dalia Lama died. Lord Buddha come in to the Tibet to renounced that the 14th Dalia Lama will be born in Amdo Taktser on 1935. Who will be changed th world.

Lord Buddha came to Tibet
Jamyang Bokto, 12 years old

This is a Tibetan Yak that live in only Tibet. Yak is very stronger than human. It is very bold and live with Tibetan in Eastern Tibet. Yak eats only grass.

A Tibetan yak
This is a Tibetan yak that lives only in Tibet.
The yak is much stronger than a man.
It is very brave and lives with Tibetans in Eastern Tibet.
The yak eats only grass.

Jamyang Bokto, 12 years old

85

A Tibetan yak
Jamyang Bokto, 12 years old

B O K T O

Jamyang Bokto was born in 1988 in India and has been at the TCV since the age of seven. His family is partly of Korean origin.

My family
There are ten members in my family: my father, my mother, my grandmother, two uncles, one aunt, three small sisters and myself.

My biggest fear
My biggest fear is at night and about my future.
And I fear to die.

My dream
In my dream Tibet was under China.
And the dragon was scaring Tibetans.
And Tibet stayed quietly under China.

86

One day I would like to be a …
… pilot - because until now no Tibetan has been a pilot
and I want to show the whole world that Tibetans are not backward.

"My dream"
Jamyang Bokto, 13 years old

From the stimulus: *Paint and write about the topic "My dream".*

In my dream, Tibet was under China, And the dragon was scaring to Tibetan, And Tibetan stayed quitly under the China.

Jamyang Bokto

Jamyang Bokto writes and paints his thoughts about Nazim Hikmet's poem as follows:

To live
Alone and free
Like a tree
And brotherly
Like a forest
Is our longing.

Nazim Hikmet[45]

88

Jamyang Bokto's text:

I am alone and…free
but I am unglad
because I wanted like to be with other
birds and go with them[46].
Original: English

[45] Nazim Hikmet was a famous Turkish lyric poet (b. 1902 in Thessaloniki, d. 1961 in Moscow)
[46] For further works by Jamyang Bokto see the following chapter

Name ~ Jamyang Bokto
Age ~ 14
Tibetan ~

To live
Alone and free
Like a tree
And brotherly
Like a forest
Is our longing

Nazim Hikmet

89

press your impressions to N.Hikmet's poem in
painting. May be you like to write an own poem!
I am alone and bored and free. But I am unglad because
wanted be other birds and go with them.

To Live
Jamyang Bokto, 14 years old

From Nazim Hikmet's
poem *To live*

What most preoccupies Tibetan children in exile today?

This question was uppermost in my mind when choosing pictures and stories for this book. During the project approximately 300 pictures and stories were created, in which the Tibetan refugee children and adolescents (from 8 to 16 years old) could give free rein to their imaginations, using stimuli taken from works of art from all over the world. The stories were written by the children in Tibetan, English or German[47].

In these works the children present the various themes in their own individual ways, and it is the aim of this publication to help the reader to create, from these kaleidoscopic descriptions, his or her own conception of the things that especially preoccupy the Tibetan children in exile today.

It was extremely difficult to make a choice because so many creative and expressive works were offered that it was not possible to reproduce all of them. All the children and indeed all who took part in the project deserve to be thanked wholeheartedly for their great commitment, especially as the work took place in their scarce free time!

As can be seen from the pictures and stories, the ethics of Tibetan Buddhism strongly influences the everyday life of these exiles from their earliest childhood. Tibetan traditions and the deeply rooted beliefs of Tibetan Buddhism continue to provide an important structure of meaning for this community. The hope of being able to return one day to their homeland is embodied in the person of the 14th Dalai Lama, who exerts a strong unifying influence and is a much loved and respected figure.

The eagerly expressed hope to be able to return one day to Tibet and the sense of a strong and enduring link with their own culture are central elements in many of the pictures and stories of the Tibetan children, regardless of their place of exile.

Each of the following parts of this chapter focuses on a particular aspect of the inner world of these children. They begin by describing their personal feelings (6.1) then their dreams and fantasies (6.2.). This is followed by the presentations focusing on religion (6.3.), nature (6.4.) and social life (6.5.). The final part (6.6.) focuses on poetry writing, something that occupies a special place in Tibetan tradition.

Tibetan children at work

The sense of being strongly rooted in their Buddhist tradition is clearly seen in the children's everyday communication with each other and with the world. This is revealed, for example, in their great willingness to help each other as well as strangers (like myself). Their openness towards the outside world is clearly manifested in their strong motivation to learn foreign languages (especially English) as well their eagerness to take part in international events in various fields of activity. Many Tibetan boys are enthusiastic about football, for example.

90

[72] The Tibetan texts are printed in German or English translation and, where possible, the Tibetan original is reproduced. In each case there is a reference to the original language. Stories written in English were "cautiously" corrected.

One thing especially worth mentioning is their extraordinary ability to concentrate on the tasks that I gave them, to immerse themselves fully in the work, often under conditions that were not very easy. Among other qualities, I was also impressed with their modesty and patience. For example, when a group of ten children had to work with one box of crayons, there was no sign of any impatience or bad temper.

These observations, gathered during the course of the project, taught me a great deal, and I often wish that ways could be found to teach our western children similar modes of behaviour. But to go into this topic further would stretch the limits of this work.

In the following texts one of the main points is the careful association with all living beings as well as with nature as a whole. This is also an essential element of the Buddhist culture.

The Tibetans in exile endure their fates with great patience and generally show non-violence. Therefore, it is not surprising that in the stories in general one can hardly find aggressive elements!

6.1. ...I think about my parents
PERSONAL FEELINGS

91

In the centre of this chapter are such feelings as longing for homeland and homesickness; feelings that are touched upon as well in many other chapters of this book. They are, for example, expressed in the description of homeland and are often characterised in a very personal way and linked with deep emotions.

It is followed by the reflections about everyday situations that in each case are of quite individual importance for the children. Thus, such topics as *Friendship* and *Family* are central in the life of every child. Especially the topic *Family* is often linked with such topics as *Longing for homeland*, as many children in exile have to grow without their families.

To perceive others and one's own self is also an important point of reference in children's development, especially for the children with the refugee fate who have to find their completely new ways in perceiving quite different surroundings and new reference people.

Once again this becomes very clear if one looks at the list of the areas covered:

- Longing for homeland/home
- Family
- Everyday thoughts
- Friendship
- Perceiving one's own self and others
- Personal strength

LONGING FOR HOMELAND/HOME

The development of the feelings in Wangchuk's text *This is Tibet* is well understandable for the readers. In the beginning he vividly describes Tibet, he then speaks about his love for Tibet and animals and in the end he expresses his profound feelings for his parents.

This is Tibet[48]

In Tibet there are many rabbits.
The majority of the rabbits are white.
In Tibet there are many different animals.
I love them.
I take care of them.
I am happy in Tibet!
My mother loves me very much.
I remember my parents.

92   Wangchuk, 12 years old, a boy, TCV Dharamsala
Original: Tibetan

[48]The stories are provided with headings to facilitate legibility for a reader. In order to render the authenticity of the text better, the heading is mainly taken from the first sentence of the respective excerpt of the story.

M Name: Wangchuk
02 School: Upper T.C.V. School
A age: 12
N nationality: Tibeten

This is Tibet
Wangchuk, 12 years old
From: "Krokodilente"

SONAM

Two stories by *Sonam* from his native village Dogpa

Sonam Wangyal writes one after the other two texts about his native village Dogpa. His first story he devotes especially to one event which is linked with yaks and nature of Tibet. He draws parallels between his own birth and the birth of one yak (both during the monsoon time). In his second story he sets a priority and speaks about the conflict with religious content.

94 **I was born in that place called Dogpa**
When I was born, it was monsoon time.
At my home there were seven yaks.
And one yak gave birth to a baby in monsoon.
So I would like to go up into the mountain with the baby yak
and my own dog called Dhondup.

Sonam Wangyal, 12 years old, a boy, TCV Dharamsala
Original: English

I was born in that place called Dogpa
Sonam Wangyal, 12 years old

From: cut up coloured paper, stuck on

Name : Sonam Wangyal
age : 12
nationality : Tibetan
address : Dharamsala boys

I was born in that place call Dogpa. when I was born that was monsoon time and my home has seven yak and one yak has born baby in monsoons so I like to go up of the mountain with baby yak and my own dog call Dhondup

Name: Sonam Wangyal
age: 12
address: T.C.V Dharamsala
nationality: Tibetan
boy

That was the Tibet country which small habitat call Dogpa. That habitat was very slow life and beautiful place. river, grassland animal and all in that. In sky there has a man who fly. Did you know? who is that? I know it is god of Budhism. which see to how Tibetan do in their life.

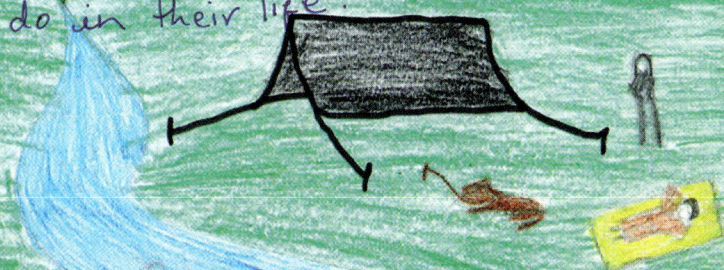

That was the Tibetan country with a small habitat called Dogpa
In that habitat there was a very slow life and it is a beautiful place. Rivers, gras-sland and animals and all that.

In the sky there is a man flying. Did you know who that is?
I know, it is the God of Buddhism, who is looking what Tibetans do in their lives.

Sonam Wangyal, 12 years old, TCV Dharamsala
Original: English

95

That was the Tibetan country…
Sonam Wangyal, 12 years old

From: "Flying Buddha", from Losel "Alternative forms of Tibetan art", Dharamsala, n.d.

A chupa and a hat made of wool… **Pasang Tashi** depicts two typical Tibetan pieces of clothes, where he uses a piece of fur for a hat and creatively decorates a chupa[49] with tiny pieces of red glittering paper. Both pieces of clothes he associates in his text with his strong feelings about Tibet.

A chupa and a hat made of wool…
When I was in Tibet I wore a chupa and a hat which is made of wool.
The colour of my chupa is brown.
At that time my hair was very long
and I am very happy in my country Tibet!

96   Pasang Tashi, 12 years old, a boy, TCV Dharamsala
Original: English

[49] *Chupa*: a traditional Tibetan dress

Name = Pasang Tashi

Age = 12

School = T.C.V. Upper

Nationality = Tibetan boy

When I was in Tibet I wears a chupa and a cap which made up by wool. My chupa colour is brown. That time my hair is very long and I am very happy in my country Tibet.

A chupa and a hat made of wool…
Pasang Tashi, 12 years old

From the stimulus:
A piece of fur and Small pieces of glittering paper

Family

After a detailed consideration of Sonam Yangzom's artistic presentation of her family one can find many common aspects that distinguish typical Tibetan refugee fates: her mother who alone has to bring up her children after the early death of her husband. Her sister and she go to the TCV in Dharamsala, one of her brothers is on the way to England to study there, the other brother lives in a monastery as a novice in Nepal, only the youngest sister still stays with her mother in Tibet!

My family comes from Kham

My mother is a housewife (39 years old).
My father Lhamo Wangyal is dead.
My sister Pema Diki is 16, she goes to the upper TCV-school.
My brother Chemi Dhondup is 21. He will study in England.
My younger sister (9 years old) is in Tibet.
I am 11 years old.
My younger brother is 10 years old, he is a pupil in Nepal.

Sonam Yangzom, 11 years old, a girl, TCV Dharamsala
Original: English

My family comes from Kham
Sonam Yangzom, 11 years old

My family live in kham

my mother
She is
h se wife
age=39

Lhamo Wangyal
Late
She goes
in upper
F.C.V.
school.

Pema Diki
Sister age=16

Chemi Dhrundup
brother age=21

Me is
going to
study
in
England.

Tulku Rinpoche
age=8

me age=11

younges
sister
age=9
she is
in
Tibet

younger
brother
age=10

Monastray
in Tibet

Me is student of
Nepal school.

In Dawa Dolma's story it expresses the joy of meeting again. From many conversations and from the content of many stories it is strongly felt again and again that the children despite all the care suffer from being away from their parents and from being able to see them very rarely (if at all!). Moreover, the joy is greater when there is a possibility to meet once again!

Once upon a time there lived a girl called Dolma
She has not seen her parents for a long time.
One day she got a telegram which said
that her parents would come to Leh at two o'clock.
100 *She was waiting for her parents near the airport.*
She saw her parents coming to her.
She was very glad to see her parents.
She clapped her hands many times.
The airport is near the garden.

Dawa Dolma, 8 years old, a girl, TCV Ladakh
Original: English

Once upon a time…
Dawa Dolma, 8 years old

From: artist's group *Die Schlumper*
"Sisyphus"

Name: Dana Dolma
age: 8 yrs old
address: s.o.s. T. C.V. school
nationality: pure Tibetan

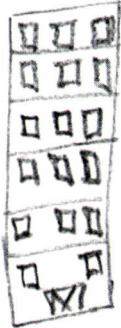

Once upon a time a girl called Dolma. she never seen her parent sincelong time one day. she got a telegram Say that her parent come to leh at 2'clock. she was wait for her parent at airport. near to parent she saw a her parent come on her side. she was very glad to see her parent. she clapped her hand many time. Air port near garden.

Everyday thoughts
Dukpa Dorje comments on the working situation from his everyday school life - an obligatory visit of the library.

Tashi is coming down from the library.
And he is going to his classroom.

Dukpa Dorje, 11 years old, a boy, TCV
Original: English

Tashi is coming up from the library...
Dukpa Dorje, 11 years old

From: artist's group *Die Schlumper*
from the series "Die Treppensteiger"
(stair climbers)

Tashi is com@ing down
from libraray. And he
is going to his class room.

In Gonpo Dorje's work his inner satisfaction is heard: he talks about a person who is sitting on a chair in the room. This person seems to be in complete harmony with his surroundings and himself.

I sit on the chair
I sit there.
It is a good year.
Many people are with Gonpo Dorje.

Gonpo Dorje, 9 years old, a boy, TCV Ladakh
Original: English

104

I sit on the chair
Gonpo Dorje, 9 years old

From: Paul Klee "Schellenengel"
(angel with a bell)

[illegible]

[illegible]

[illegible]

[illegible]

[illegible]

[illegible]

Friendship

Tenzin, who lives in Switzerland, describes the development of one deep friendship between two girls who come from different countries. In the final sentence of her story she probably makes a link to her own situation:

With this story I want to say that children also can be friends in other countries.

Two inseparable friends

Once Veronica wanted to go to Africa with her family.
They lived in Germany.
...When they were in Africa, they wanted to go to the market.
Cori worked at the market. She sold fruits.
Veronica came up with her family to this stall.
First they talked about fruits,
and then Veronica asked her where she lived.
She said "On the beach!"
The next day they wanted to meet each other again.
They always went together.
They were inseparable.
That was it. Veronica had to go back to Germany.
Veronica didn't want it, she wanted to stay for some weeks longer...

With this story I want to say that children also can be friends in other countries.

Tenzin, 13 years old, a girl, Rikon, Switzerland
Original: German

106

Two inseparable friends
Tenzin, 13 years old

From: Siberian cave-painting

TENZIN

བོད།

Tibet

Cori

Veronika

ཚེ་ཞིའི་བདེ་ལེགས།

Greetings (Tashi Delek)

Tenzin Tsomo is in conflict with the mother's ban. A boy secretly meets his friend although his mother doesn't allow it but the boy in her story expressively emphasises that he is *very happy*!

Once there was a boy whose name was Dhundup
He was worried because his mother told him
not to play with his friend.
And then his mother went to the market.
And immediately he went down the stairs.
And his friend Dorje met him there.
Then Dhundup was very happy.

108   Tenzin Tsomo, 8 years old, a girl, TCV Ladakh
Original: English

Once there was a boy whose name was
Dhundup
Tenzin Tsomo, 8 years old

From: artist's group *Die Schlumper* from the
series "Die Treppensteiger" (stair climbers)

Perceiving one's own self and others

Lobsang Dolker presents simple facts about perceiving and comparing others and one's own self.

One day the man was on his way

He saw a bird:
He was surprised:

Because the colour of his face was the same as of the bird,
and the wings of the bird were purple.

Lobsang Dolker, 10 years old, a girl, TCV Ladakh
Original: English

One day the man was going he saw a bird. He was surprised to bird. because, His face colour was same to bird and the bird wing colour was the perpa

One day the man was on his way
Lobsang Dolker, 10 years old

From: Paul Klee "Schellenengel" (Angel with a bell)

Ngawang Jampa develops his ideas about one beautiful well-built woman from India. It strikes him that her husband is physically smaller than she is, *but he is good at work and everything else*.

By the way a small piece of red paper from which Ngawang Jampa makes a small red handbag for the woman is the starting point for his picture.

This woman is from India…
…and she lives with her husband who is very short.
But he is very good at work and everything else.
But she is very tall and very nice.
She always takes her small red bag with her.

112 Ngawang Jampa, 14 years old, a boy, TCV Dharamsala,
Original: English

This woman is from India
Ngawang Jampa, 14 years old
(Dharamsala)

From a piece of red coloured paper

Name: Ngawang Sangpo
age: 14
address: T.C.V. school
nationality: Tibetan

This woman is Indain and she lived with her husband who was very short but he is very good in work or anything But she is very tall and very nice. She always take her small red bag with her.

113

Within this collection Chemie Namgyal speaks about rather rarely discussed topic. It concerns conflict resolution. It is left open whether and how the conflict began. The small man indeed asked about the reason for reproaching him; hierarchy however remained untouched.

A warning
That big man gives a warning to a small man.
"Why?" a small man asks him in the market.
The big man warns the small man again.
"These warnings are given because you threw something there…"

Chemie Namgyal, 12 years old, a boy, TCV Ladakh
114 Original: English

A warning
Chemie Namgyal, 12 years old

From: Leonardo da Vinci "Gesichtsstudien"
(facial studies)

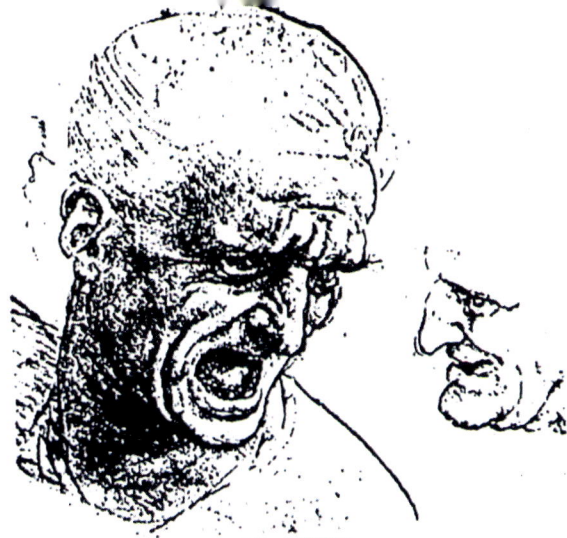

That big man worning to small man
why they small man then in
market then for they big
man worning to small man.
That worning is you then
a thing.

115

Personal strength

The reflections in various forms that present personal strength belong to the development of one's personality. Thus, Tenzin Deydhen and Tenzin Gatop give different interpretations of the image of *Sisyphus*[50] that both deal with the overall aspect of the development and use of personal strength.

Tenzin Deydhen is guided in general by the legend about Sisyphus from Greek mythology. For him it is about achieving something (*to take this heavy rock to the top...*), the end is left open.

The aim

He has a real power to take this heavy rock to the top of the mountain.
So he is trying to take this heavy rock to the top.
That's his aim.

116

Tenzin Deydhen, 12 years old, a boy, TCV Ladakh
Original: English

The aim
Tenzin Deydhen, 12 years old

From: artist's group *Die Schlumper* "Sisyphus"

[50] *Sisyphus* (Lat.): In Greek mythology a hero who was exiled into the underworld. As a punishment for his cheating Sisyphus was condemned to roll up a heavy rock stone onto the mountain in the underworld, but it always rolled backwards before reaching the top. According to this legend, a laborious activity that does not lead to any success is called *Sisyphean task* (www.beyars.com/kunstlexikon/lexikon_8370.html)

e has a real power
take this heavy rock
the top of mountain. So,
was trying to take this heavy
ock to the top. that's his aim.

For Tenzin Gatop Sisyphus figure is using all its power to avert danger, to prevent something. He is closely attached to the phenomenon from his surroundings: in the mountainous world of the Himalayas it often happens that pieces of rock come off and fall onto the roads.

...*stop the stone from rolling down*
Once upon a time there was a man,
he was going on holiday.
The man was so happy about his place in the mountains.
He saw that on the mountain there was a very big stone.
He stopped the stone from rolling down and helped
that the road was not blocked.
Then he went home and enjoyed...

Tenzin Gatop, 12 years old, a boy, TCV Ladakh
Original: English

118

119

6.2. *In my dreams…*
DREAMS AND FAIRY-TALES

Dreams and descriptions with fairy-tale content are the essential topics about which many children write.

These topics were taken up either to present dreams the children really experienced, and to develop them a bit further or to make dreadful projections and fantasies, for example, to express one's own feelings, wishes and fears.

Therefore, I took up the topic *My dream* and in addition offered it as a stimulus for writing and painting[51].

Fairy-tale dreams

A fairy-tale description of a mythical creature by Thupten Tsering concerns the topic *Fear*. The creature (a she-giant) is described in all details and is vividly presented. Shortly after the dramatic climax (*…she -* the princess - *fell down on the way*) everything proves to be like in a bad dream!

The giant

Once upon a time there was a girl who was a princess.
One day she was going back to her home.
Suddenly the weather changed into dark.
Then she was so frightened.
Suddenly in the forest she saw a horrible giant,
who was a princess of the giant of the forest.
She saw that the giant had wings
and her eyes were on the wings and on the back.
She had five eyes and also a horn on her head.
She was very much afraid and she fell down on the way.
At last all that was her dream.

Thupten Tsering, 13 years old, a girl, TCV Dharamsala
Original: English

120

The giant
Thupten Tsering, 13 years old

From: Pablo Picasso "Stierkopf" (bull's head)

[51] Cf. e.g. the presentation of the dreams of the four children from the TCV Dharamsala

Once upon a time There was a girl who is princess

Dreams

Thoughts about Tibet make up a central topic just as if it were about a wishful dream or a nightmare.

Dreams also reflect the subjects which are discussed in other chapters (thus, the topic *Dreams* often overlaps with the topic *Longing for homeland*). In the chapter *Poems* it is also frequently mentioned about longings and wishful dreams.

Every time during these three years Ngawang Migmar chooses this topic and describes his dreams. When he was 13 years old he had an unusual idea to interpret Leonardo da Vinci's "Gesichtsstudien" as a fictitious dialogue between Gandhi and German President about Tibet. One year later he described a sketch by Marc Chagall as a return to his homeland. In his dream he achieves this by wings. A further year later he associates it again with a fictitious meeting and get-together on the basis of one poem by the Turkish writer Nazim Hikmet.

What a big longing for his family and his homeland must be in this child…!

122

In my dream…
Ngawang Migmar, 13 years old

From: Leonardo da Vinci "Gesichtsstudien" (facial studies)

Name: Ngawang Migmar
age: 13
address: upper T.C.V.
nationality: Tibetan

In my dream, Gandi and German Presentend were talking about Tibetan.

I have a dream…
*…that I have wings and I am going
to fly to catch a bird.
But I cannot catch the bird.
Suddenly I reach my country.
I think it is all real.
But it is a dream.
So I want to go to my country Tibet.*

Ngawang Migmar, 14 years old,
TCV Dharamsala
Original: English

124

*I have a dream…
Ngawang Migmar, 13 years old*

From: Franz Meyer "Marc Chagall Leben und Werk" Du Mont. Schauberg Köln. 61, S. 380

I have a dream that I am I had wings and I am going to ~~catch~~ fly to catch bird. But I can not catch the bird. Suddenly I reach my country. I thing it is a realy. But It is dream. So I want to go te my country Tibet.

Ngawang Migmar
H = 36 School = Upper T.C.V
Class VII O age = 15

To live
Alone and free
Like a tree
And brotherly
Like a forest
Is our longing

Nazim Hikmet

Is this dream we lived togeather.

I am home happy to meet you all

In this dream…
…we all live together.
I am very happy to meet you all.

Ngawang Migmar, 14 years old,
TCV Dharamsala
Original: English

125

In this dream…
Ngawang Migmar, 15 years old
(Dharamsala)

From: Nazim Hikmet *To live* (a poem)

Express your impressions to N. Hikmet's poem in a painting. May be you like to write an own poem!

Up in to the mountain, push me not
When ever you go, forget me not

Konchok Aka formulates an archaic fearful dream (*the world is dark and the dragons are flying over the ocean…*), while Tenzin Wangchuk in his dream touches upon the topic *Sponsor* in quite a humorous way: most of all he likes sponsors in Paris and London and would also like to be there but he writes as well *if I were in Tibet, I go to my parents…*

This is my dream
A very fearful dream.
The world was dark and the dragons were flying through the ocean.
The ocean water was splashing to the walls.
I was so feared that I woke up.
The dream disappeared.

126

Konchok Aka, 13 years old, a boy, TCV Dharamsala
Original: English

This is my dream
Konchok Aka, 13 years old

From the stimulus: ornaments from Asian brocade

Name : Konchok Aka
age : 13
nationality : Tibetan
address : UPPER T. C. V. school.

This is my dream. A very fear ~~dream~~ dream. The world was dark and dragons were flying through ocean. The ocean water was spashing to the walls. When I was so fear ~~and~~ that I woke up. ~~and~~ the dream disipeared.

In my dream…
If I were in Tibet, I want go with my parents.
If I went to Paris, I would see my sponsor and his wife.
If I were in London, I would see my other sponsor and go
with him.
It?s all in my dream…

Tenzin Wangchuk, 12 years old, a boy, TCV Dharamsala
Original: English

In my dream…
Tenzin Wangchuk, 12 years old

WANGCHUK

In my Dream,

If I were In Tibet

I want to go with my parent

If I went to

the the Paris I saw my sponsor

and his wife. If I were in London

If saw my another sponsor and so with

him. Its all in my Dream

129

NGAWANG

In his dream Ngawang Jampa touches upon pictures of his homeland, topics which we frequently come across in this book always appearing in new connections.

This is my dream…
…and in my dream I am in Tibet with my parents.
I look after yaks and
I always ride on a yak which is my best yak.
It?s colour is black and it has long horns.

Ngawang Jampa, 14 years old, a boy, TCV Dharamsala
Original: English

130

This is my dream…
Ngawang Jampa, 14 years old

From: Pablo Picasso "Stierkopf" (bull's head)

JAMPA

This is my dream
and in my dream
I am in the Tibet
with parents. I
looked after yaks and
I always riding
on a yak which is
my best yak. Its color is
buich and it has longhorns.

Tashi Dhondup finally touches upon the topic *Religion* and moves onto the next chapter, in which this subject is emphasised by pictures and stories.

In my dream I was going to heaven…
…because before I studied Buddhism and
I became a holy man like great H.H. the Dalai Lama.
I renew (?) the peace for the world and I go to heaven.

Tashi Dondup, 14 years old, a boy, TCV Dharamsala
Original: English

132

In my dream I was going to heaven…
Tashi Dhondup, 14 years old

From: "Flying Buddha", Losel "Alternative forms of Tibetan art", Dharamsala, n.d.

Name: Tashi Dhondup
age: 14.
address: T.C.V. School
nationality: Tibetan

133

In my dream I was going into the heaven because this before I study Bubbist and I became a holy man like great H. H. the Dalai Lhama. I renounce the peace for world and I go to heaven.

by. Tashi Dhondup.
6111

6.3.   *Our Lamas are so great…*
RELIGION

Tenzin Tsokji, made quite an original head cover of one Nyingmapa-Lama[52] from a piece of red glittering paper. Her text reminds one of a song of praise of the Tibetan Lama. She takes pride in her cultural heritage, which is evidently felt in her lines.

Nyingmapa Lama
This is our country's Lama.
He is great.
Every day they are praying all day long.
Our Tibetan Lamas are so great.
Lamas have a lot of pity.
Many Lamas are in Tibet.

134

Tenzin Tsokji, 12 years old, a girl, TCV Dharamsala
Original: English

Nyingmapa Lama
Tenzin Tsokji, 12 years old

From the stimulus: a piece of red glittering paper

[52] *Nyingmapas*: one of the four main traditions in Tibetan Buddhism (Gelugpa, Kagyu, Nyingmapa, Sakyia). The Nyingmapa-school, also called *School of the Old*, puts its emphasis on the magic and mystic practice of Lamaism. In the original the hat of Lama in Nyingmapas is made of silk damask and silk brocade damask (cf. timphubhuthan.at:81)

Name: Tenzin Tsokyi
Age: 12
address: upper T.C.V school
nationality: Tibetan

This is our
Country's lama
monk. It is great.

Everyday they
praying all day.

NYING
MA
PA
L AME

Our Tibets lamas are so great. lama are
so pity. Many lamas are in Tibet.

135

Lobsang Chokey tries to present in simple words what he has understood about the importance of prayers in Buddhism. Such aspects as *karma* and *reincarnation* are indicated.

Once upon a time there was a man called Tashi
He is a Tibetan.
He is always playing with his beads[54] to overcome his luck.
He believes that it will be helpful to him to vanish his bad sins and others.
When he dies, he can take his good deeds (with him).

Lobsang Chokey, 14 years old, a boy,
Kathmandu, Nepal
Original: English

136

Once upon a time there was a man called Tashi
Lobsang Chokey, 14 years old

From: Paul Klee's sketch from "Senecio"

[54] The pearls of *Mala* are meant
(the prayer chain consisting of 108 pearls)

nationality: Tibetan
School: kedong Thuk-che choling
boy
girl   girl

TENZIN

Tenzin Choesan finally speaks about the importance of the enormous *Vajras* in front of the SwajambuNath-Stupa and conveys factual information about these tantric ritual objects.

Once I went to visit SwajambuNath-Stupa
There I saw a big Vajra which attracted me very much.
And I was curious to know about it and I asked the people
about it which is as following:
"Vajra/ Diamond, (…) sceptre,
a symbol of strength and indestructibility,
also a tantric ritual object consisting of cylindrical axis
from which two sets of curved spoxes radiate".

Tenzin Choesang, 13 years old, a girl, Kathmandu, Nepal
Original: English

138

Once I went to visit Swajambu Nath-Stupa
Tenzin Choesang, 13 years old

From: Lavizzari-Raeuber (89)

CHOESAN

Name:
Tenzin
Choesang

age: 13

Once I went to visit SwayambhuNath Stupa. There I saw a big vajra which attracted me very much. And I was curious to know about it and I asked the people about it which is as following:

Vajra / Diarmond hard, adamantime Sceptre, a Symbol of strength and indestructibity, also a tantric ritual object consisting of a cylinclinchical axis from which two sets of curved spokes radiate.

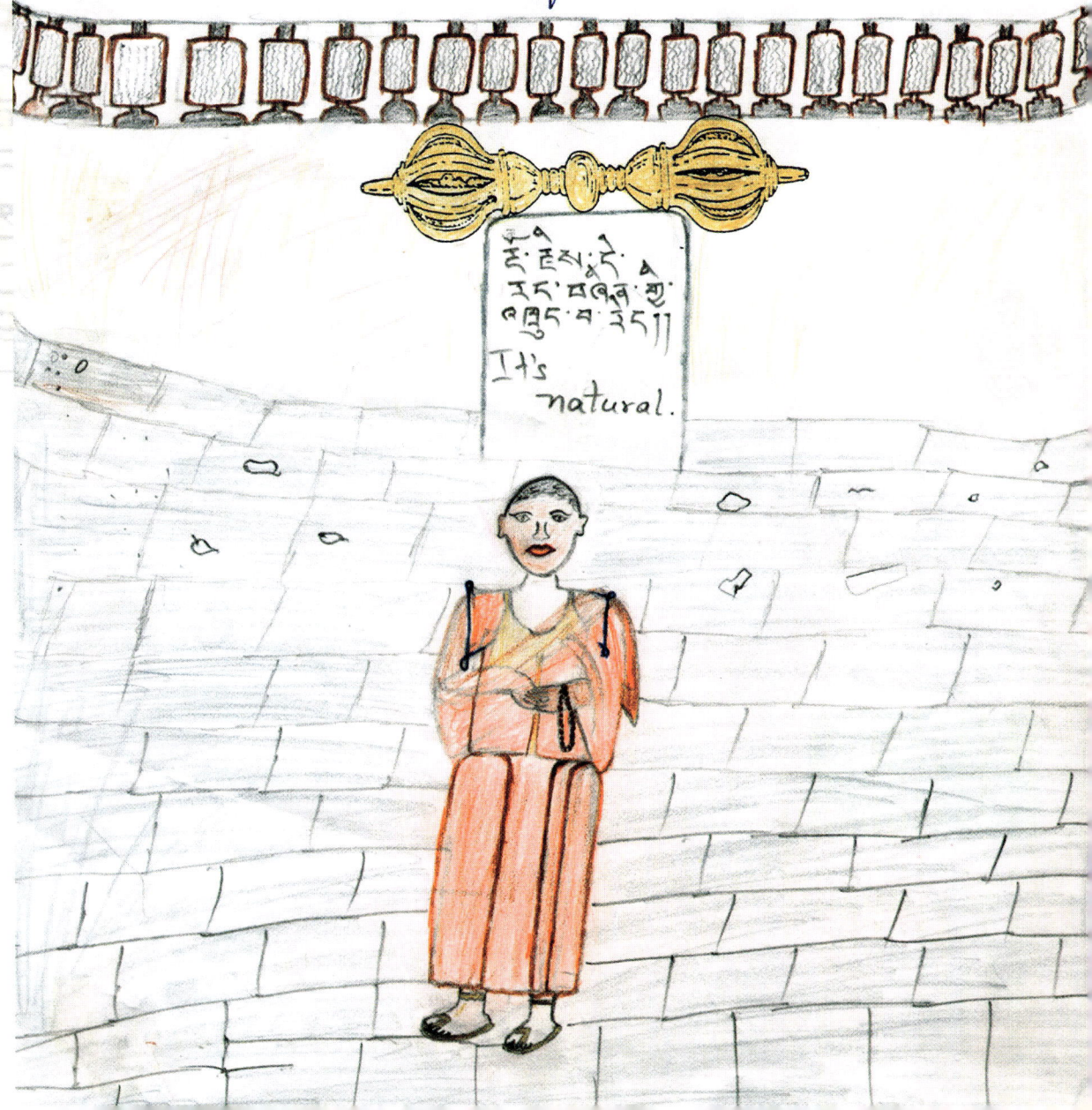

ཧ་ཧས་དེ་
རད་བཞིན་གྱི་
འགྱུར་བ་རེད།།

It's natural.

Urgen Togyal and Tenzin Thokman present their personal
visions about "heaven"[55]

A fairy flying high up in the sky
The figure in the picture is supposed to be a fairy
flying high up in the sky.
After practicing religious rituals for sometime,
She has gained special power to fly, but soon she realized
That there is no true peace in just flying in the sky.

Urgen Topgyal, 8 years old, a boy, TCV Ladakh
Original: Tibetan

140

This is God
Urgen Topgyal, 8 years old

From: "Flying Buddha", Losel "Alternative
forms of Tibetan art", Dharamsala, n.d.s.

[55]Here only presented as pictures

To practice Buddhism
It is essential for all Tibetans to practice Buddhism.
The person (flying) in the drawing, has reached heaven
Because of his intense spiritual practice.
Even I wanted to practice Buddhism,
in order to be in heaven within this lifetime.
If not, I will succeed in my next life.

Tenzin Thokmon, 11 years old, a boy, TCV Ladakh
Original: Tibetan

142

...I read prayers and I'm going to heaven...
Tenzin Thokman, 11 years old

From: "Flying Buddha", Losel "Alternative
forms of Tibetan art", Dharamsala, n.d.s.

Name: Tenzin Tholmon
age: 11
address: SOS T.C.V school, p/o choglamsar.
nationality: Tibetan

ཁྱོད་ཀྱི་ཡུལ།

FREE TIBET.

6.4. *The map of Tibet is very beautiful…*
NATURE

The first part concerns some general ideas about nature and environmental protection worldwide, especially about the conflict and fear for the consequences of the environment which is becoming increasingly destroyed (*Nature and environmental protection*). The stories in which the aspects of modern technology are discussed are related to this.

The subjects *Nature and environmental protection* correspond to the central Buddhist fundamental ideas. The development of sympathy for all living beings in Buddhism is inseparably linked with these items.

In the second part the children are preoccupied with the description of the nature of their homeland Tibet. An important part is devoted to their native animals, first of all, yaks as well as bees and snakes etc., they motivate the children to imagine their own stories.

To feel and identify oneself with nature and the world of animals of Tibet this main idea of Tibetan Buddhism is an essential constant topic of the stories that comes up in various facets (as a real description, in the form of fables or fairy-tales).

Nature and environmental protection
Jigmet Lhundup presents a picture, a landscape of Tibet.

A clean place…
Jigmet Lhundup, 8 years old

From: "Flying Buddha", Losel "Alternative forms of Tibetan art", Dharamsala, n.d.s.

144

Name: Jigmet Lhundup
age: eight
address: T.C.V LADAKH
nationality: LADAKHI

NGAWANG

Ngawang Jampa speaks about the maintenance of nature and the responsibility of the people for it and urgently warns about the destruction of the environment.

If we don't keep our mother Earth clean…
…the garbage ocean will cover our nice place.
We must keep our Earth clean
and we must not cut our nice plants and trees.
The trees are the most important things we have.
If there are no trees,
we won't be there too.

Ngawang Jampa, 14 years old, a boy, TCV Dharamsala
Original: English

146

If we don't keep our Mother Earth clean,
Ngawang Jampa, 14 years old

From: Katashika Hokusai "Fujijama"

JAMPA

Name : Ngawang Tampa
age 14
nationality Tibetan
School T.C.V. School
boy ✓
girl

If we dont keep our mother earth clean. The garbage ocean will cover our nice place. We must keep our earth clean and we do not cut our nice plants and trees. The trees are most important things we have. If the trees are not there and we are not there too.

Tenchok writes a two-part story: while in the first part he describes *the old times*, when the environment wasn't destroyed yet and the world of animals and plants co-existed in harmony, in his second part he paints a fearful vision of the future of the completely destroyed environment.

Picture A

Before a time animals enjoyed their life very much
and were glad.
Because the environment was very clean and lots of trees
gave us oxygen.
No one can cut a tree and kill an animal.
Our Earth has lots of rivers.

Picture B

In future time there will be no trees on the Earth,
that is why animals don't get oxygen and food.
The sun is very hot and will dry all the rivers,
and we won't get any water.
All these are the reasons and one day all living beings will die.

Tenchok, 13 years old, a boy, TCV Dharamsala
Original: English

Picture A, Picture B
Tenchok, 13 years old

From: Katashika Hokusai "Fujijama"

boy = boy
girl

Figure 'A'
Before a time, animal
spend life very injoy
and glad. because
enviroment are very
clean and lots of
tree and gives us
oxygen. No one can
cut the tree and kill
the animal. the Our
earth have lots
of river

Figure 'A'

Figure 'B'
Future time no trees in
the earth that ways animal
have don²t got oxygen and
food. The sun is very
hot and dried all the river
and don²t got water. There
all the reason and one d
all the living things are
died.

Figure 'B'

Dawa Tsomo also devotes her thoughts to the welfare of the world as a whole. The starting point for her is her *Motherland*…

I am thinking about our Motherland
To keep the world clean -
So that's why I am thinking about the world.

Dawa Tsomo, 13 years old, a girl, TCV Dharamsala
Original: English

150

I am thinking about our motherland
Dawa Tsomo, 13 years old

From: Valery Bugrov "Heaven and Earth", 1991

T S O M O

Name: Dawa Tsomo
age: 13
address (upper) T.C.V School
nationality: Tibetan
Girl

I am thinking about our motherland. To clean the world so thats why I am thinking about the world

Modern technology

The following stories are devoted to the world of technology, real and fictional. They present an acute contrast to the description of nature, and this is made deliberately to explain the wide spectre of the children's interests. For example, the story by Tenzin Woesel is devoted to the future research of space.

This space rocket is very powerful

This rocket is made in the USA.
The rocket is going into the space.

Tenzin Woesel, 13 years old, a boy, TCV Dharamsala
Original: English

152

This space rocket is very powerful
Tenzin Woesel, 13 years old

From: small pieces of coloured paper

Name = Tenzin Woesel

age = 13

nationality = Tibetan

address = TCV School Upper.

E.T.

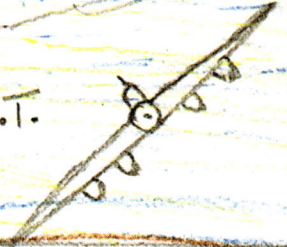

1|8|2000

This SPACE Rocket is very powerfull.

This Rocket is made in U.S.A. Rocket is going to space.

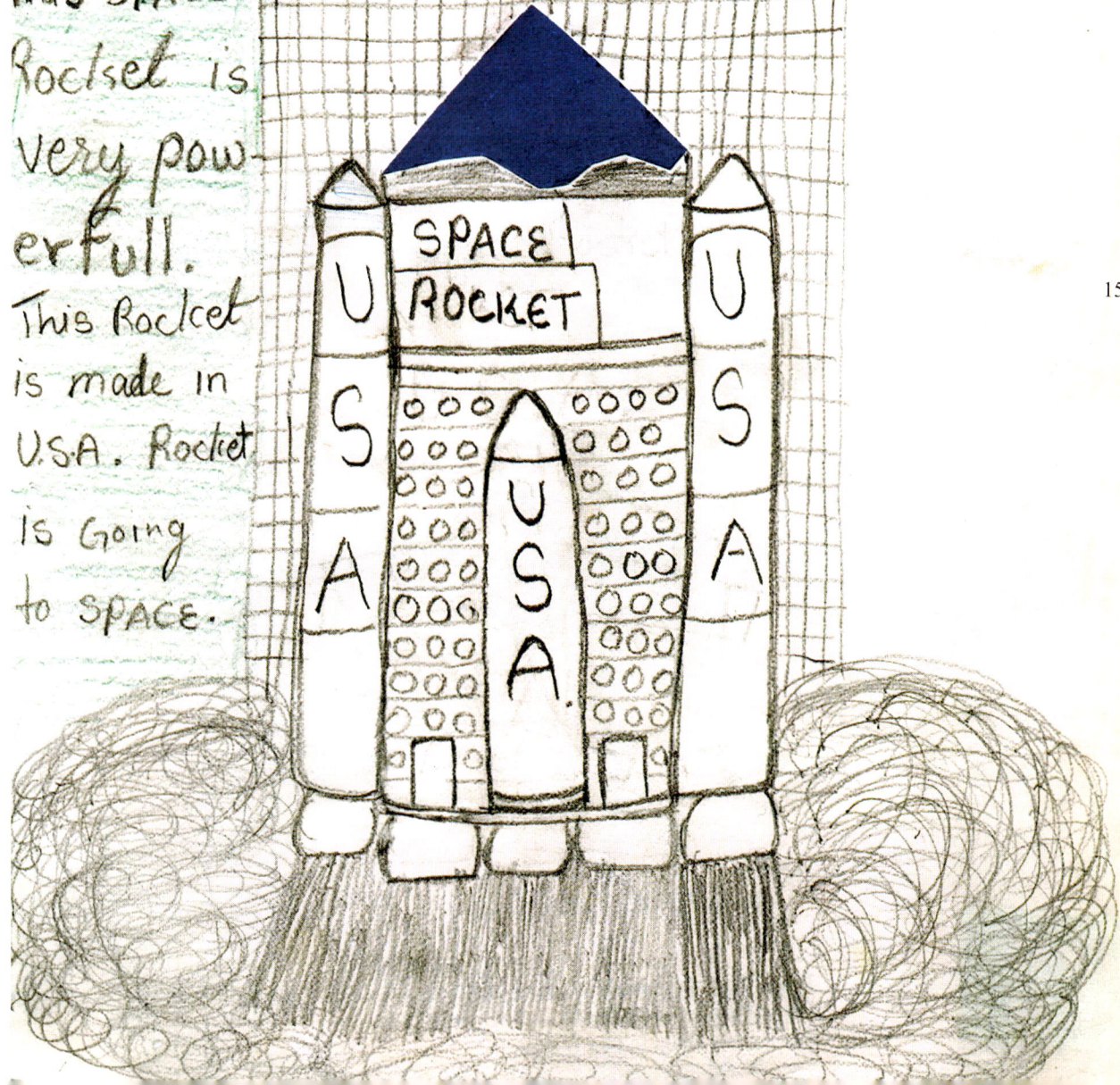

SPACE ROCKET

USA

USA

USA

153

Tenzin Tenkyong integrates science fiction in his story: a robot as a servant in his private life.

He is a robot or a servant of mine

He can make tea for us and he always plays cricket with me. His foot has seven wheels for each (foot), left and right. He can also talk and he is my best friend in the world. He is made by my father.

Tenzin Tenkyong, 8 years old, a boy, TCV Dharamsala
Original: English

He is a robot or a servant of mine
Tenzin Tenkyong ,8 years old

He is a robert or the servent of mine.
He can make tea for us and he always play
cricet with me. His foot has seven wheel
for each left and right. He can also talk and
he is my best friend in the world. he is
made by my father

Topgyal's story also concerns a fictional creature (*a mixture of an animal and a tree*), which at first he describes in detail. Finally he links it with his fantastic thought about ecology and gives a final warning for the use of too many technologies.

"It" - from outer planets

It is a mixture of many animals and trees and
they do not eat food and make their own food inside their body.
On it?s head bull's horns and hair (...) is mixed.
Their airplane has wings like bird?s wings.
If one day the living beings on the Earth change into such beings,
This is because they use too many technologies,
and our ecology will become very fearful.
So that's why we should use less technologies
and save trees to live in peace.

Topgyal, 13 years old, a boy, TCV Dharamsala
Original: English

"It"- from outer planets
Topgyal, 13 years old

From: small pieces of coloured paper

157

Tsundue Dolma's fantastic creature from Mercury finally starts an (unsuccessful) trial to steal the whole Earth in order to enrich itself on its water supplies!

Once upon a time there was a man
He came from other space (Mercury) and wanted to get our Earth away.
Because there is no water on the Mercury, he came here to get it.
But he couldn't put it on the mountain because he had an oxygen cylinder on his back and the Earth is very heavy.

Tsundue Dolma, 12 years old, a girl, TCV Dharamsala
Original: English

Once upon a time there was a man
Tsundue Dolma, 12 years old

From: artist's group *Die Schlumper* "Sisyphus"

159

Once upon a time there was
a man He was from other space (Mer-
ury) to get our earth because.
in Mercury there are no water that
why he came to get). But he cant
able to pul it on the mountain beca
use he took oxygen cylinder at back
and earth awar very heavy.

The nature of Tibet

Dawa Tsomo and Tenzin Jigmey describe the beauty of the nature of Tibet: Dawa Tsomo glances at the life of the Tibetan nomads who live in tents that are made from yaks' skins, and Tenzin Jigmey outlines numerous beauties of Tibetan nature on the map of Tibet.

Our country Tibet

In Tibet they have tents made from yaks' skins.
In these tents nomads live.
They keep animals like yaks and horses.

Dawa Tsomo, 13 years old, a girl, TCV Dharamsala
Original: English

Our country Tibet
Dawa Tsomo, 13 years old

TSOMO

Name = Dawa Tsomo

Age = 13

Addres = U.T.C.V

Nationality = Tibetan

Girl

OUR COUNTRY
Tibet
IN Tibet They have Tent, made by yak's Skin. 再In this tent they live nomad. =)

They keep animal like Yak; hores.

It is a map of Tibet
This map is the map of Tibet.
The map of Tibet is very beautiful.
In Tibet there are many trees and much water(...).
On the map there are many mountains, yaks and sheep.
The sheep, yaks and mountains are beautiful.
The trees have many apples.

Tenzin Jigmey, 8 years old, a boy, TCV Ladakh
Original: English

162

It is a map of Tibet
Tenzin Jigmey, 8 years old

From: Valery Bugrov, a sketch from
"Heaven and Earth", 1991

163

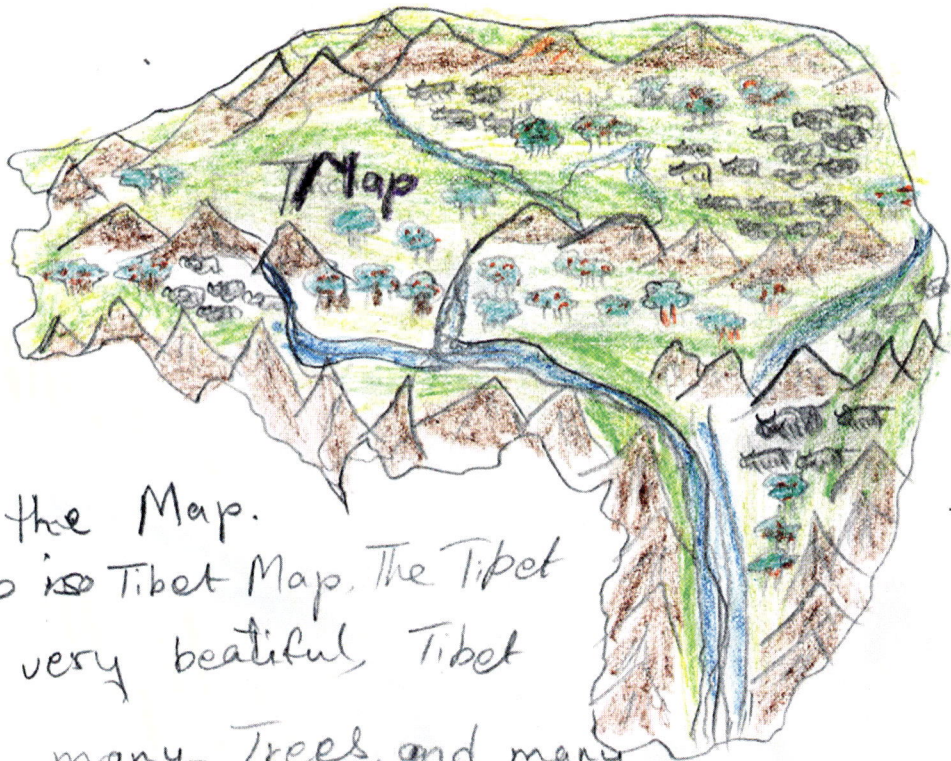

It is the Map.
This Map is Tibet Map. The Tibet
Map is very beatiful, Tibet
Map has many Trees, and many
water, But Trees colour is grand, Map has many mountine
and many yaks and many sheeps, sheep and yak and
montine it beatiful, Trees has many Appele,

Tashi Dhondup describes incessant monsoon rains in Dharamsala, the place of exile, and makes thick monsoon clouds on his picture with pieces of fur.

Here in Dharamsala the weather is very funny
In the mornings it rains and when it stops the sun is shining.
Dharamsala is a very good and high place up in a clean environment.
But we hate this rain!

Tashi Dondup, 14 years old, a boy, TCV Dharamsala
Original: English

164

Here in Dharamsala the weather is very funny
Tashi Dhondup, 14 years old

From: pieces of fur

DHONDUP

Name: Tashi Dhondup
age: 14
address: T.C.V School
nationality: Tibetan

Here in Dharamsala, the weather very funny.
At morning rain and after it stop and sun shine.
Dharamsala is very good and high place on clean
enviroment. But we hate this rain.

The world of animals

As already mentioned the description of the animal's world in Tibet is an extremely popular topic with many children. First of all yaks are described in diverse ways as well as bees and snakes.

- Yaks

The yak for a Tibetan is an important basis of life[56]

It is supposed that the yak was domesticated by the highlanders for over 2000 years. The bull is called by the Tibetans a "yak" and the female is called a "dri".

Milk products, especially butter made from the fat milk of a dri, are important basic foods of the Tibetans. The meat dried in the air is taken for long trips. Shoes are made from tanned skins, nomads weave their tents from the long hair of yaks' tails. They weave and sew chupas from the shorter hair on the stomach. A yak carries weight up to one hundred kilos through the snow and glaciers. The settled peasants put a yak into a plough. Its dung is collected and used instead of fire wood.

Three children and three different associations to the topic y*ak*:
While Ngawang Thokmey gives rather factual information about a yak, Dasa Tsomo's detailed description includes emotional nuances
(*...I love yaks very much*).

Yaks are the main animals of Tibet
Yaks can be females and males.
Females are called "dri" and males are called "yak".
Yaks are used for transporting things in Tibet:
Salt - in the main.

Ngawang Thokmey, 12 years old, a boy, TCV Ladakh
Original: English

166

Yaks are the main animals of Tibet
Ngawang Thokmey, 12 years old

From: Pablo Picasso "Stierkopf" (bull's head)

[56] Cf. in the following: Grieder, Peter "Tibet land between Heaven and Earth"

yaks are the main animal of tibet
yaks can be in female and male.
female are called Dri and male are
called yak yak is used for transporting
things and majority salt in tibet.

Yaks live in cold places like Tibet, Ladakh and Manali.
Yaks are helpful animals.
We get milk from yaks.
We make butter from their milk.
Yaks have much much fur.
Brown, white and black are the colours of yaks.
Yaks are very beautiful and the most wonderful animals in the world.
Yaks work as hard as they can.
Food of yaks is grass and water.
Yaks are strong animals.
I love yaks very much!

Dawa Tsomo, 13 years old, a girl, TCV Dharamsala
Original: English

168

I love yaks very much!
Dawa Tsomo, 13 years old

From: Pablo Picasso "Stierkopf" (bull's head)

Name: Dawa Tsomo
age: 13
address: T.C.V. school (upper)
nationality: Tibetan
Girl

Yak

Yak lives in cold ~~please~~
place like Tibet, Ladakh and
Manali Yak is helpful
animal. From yak we get a
milk. We make ~~milk~~ milk into

169

Tenzin Tsokyi touches upon the topic *Birth and Joys of Motherhood* and expresses the loving feelings of a mother-to-child relationship, concerning a mother-animal and its baby. She projects her own situation onto a yak-mother (the girl lives without her family in the TCV).

Once there was a yak-mother
She didn't have a family.
Her stomach has a baby.
Every day she sat on the grass and she ate the grass.
One day she had the baby outside from her stomach.
Mother-yak was very happy.
170 *Then the baby-yak and the mother-yak played together.*
They are very happy with their own life.

Tenzin Tsokyi, 12 years old, a girl, TCV Dharamsala
Original: English

Once there was a yak-mother
Tenzin Tsokyi, 12 years old

From: Pablo Picasso "Ziege" (the goar)

Name: Tenzin Tsokyi
age = 12
nationality = Tibet
School = Upper T.C.V school.
boy
girl = Girl

Pablo Picasso

171

Once there was yak mother. She does not have family. Her stomach has baby. Every day she ▮ sat on grass and she eat grass. One day have a baby outside from stomach. Mother yak was very happy. Then baby yak and mother yak play together. They are very happy ▮ there own life.

The End

Bees

Tenzin Paljar discusses the destruction of a beehive and as a consequence of this he expresses the girl's harm because she is stung (cause and condition!). At the end Tenzin presents the moral of the story.

Do not destroy the house of animals -
from this you can suffer a lot!

Do not destroy the house of animals

Two girls destroyed the honeybee-house.
The bees became very angry and at least one girl was bitten
all over her body by bees, and all her body was wounded.
Do not destroy the house of animals from this you can
suffer a lot!

172

Tenzin Paljar, 11 years old, a boy, TCV Ladakh
Original: English

Do not destroy the house of animals
Tenzin Paljar, 11 years old

From: "Siberian cave-painting"
Losel "Alternative forms of Tibetan art",
Dharamsala, n.d.

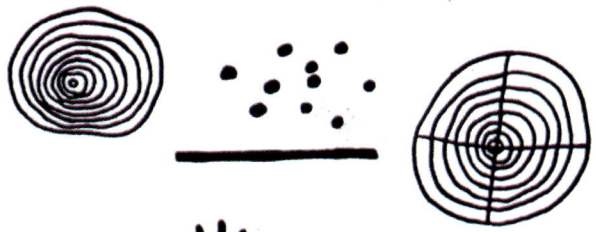

Snakes

Tenzin Dekyi's story deals with the topic *Hunger*. She gives human features to a snake and addresses it in a humorous way as *Mr.Snake*.

Mr.Snake

Mr. Snake wants to go into that house and have some lunch.
As he hasn't got any food for many days.

Tenzin Dekyi, 11 years old, a girl, TCV Ladakh
Original: English

174

Mr.Snake
Tenzin Dekyi, 11 years old

From: "Flying Buddha", Losel "Alternative forms of Tibetan art", Dharamsala, n.d.

MR snake wants to go into that house and having some lunch. As he has't got any food from many days.

Tsewang Dhundup's story concerns a mother-to-child relationship like in Tenzin Tsokij's story. This time a mother defends her child very fearlessly and successfully against the danger from the outside (*lynxes*).

The snake

Once upon a time there was a mother of a snake.
She had two children.
One day her two children were playing under a tree
when suddenly two squirrels came up and wanted to
eat the children of the snake.
Mother snake came closer ready to fight.
Both squirrels got afraid and went back to their home.

176

Tsewang Dhundup, 10 years old, a boy, TCV Ladakh
Original: English

The snake
Tsewang Dhundup, 10 years old

From: "Flying Buddha",
Losel "Alternative forms of Tibetan art",
Dharamsala n.d.

SNAKE

6.5. *Let there be peace on Earth.*
SOCIAL LIFE

A multitude of pictures and stories are linked with the conflicts covering socio-political subjects. Partly they concern some specific situations of the Tibetan refugees in exile e.g. thoughts about Mahatma Gandhi and about the present political situation in Tibet. For the Tibetans Gandhi is close to the Dalai Lama as an important symbol and first of all as a forerunner of non-violent resistance.

Some stories refer directly to the political situation in Tibet and the politics of China is commented on and criticised, however this is not done in a polemic form.

General reflections about politics, work and free time differ little from the way of thinking of other children (thus, for example, children from all over the world love football as a hobby in their free time, regardless of their origin).

The content which characterises the specific surroundings of the exile country becomes clearer in some stories (especially the topic *Work*, where a depressing description of poverty in developing countries is often touched upon)

178

Gandhi

Tenzin Kalden and Tenzin Wangmo link Leonardo da Vinci's "Gesichtsstudien" to the thoughts about their great image of Mahatma Gandhi. Tenzin Kalden sees him as a great speaker at a press conference where he supports peace in the world; Tenzin Wangmo gives some details from Gandhi's biography in two languages (Tibetan and English).

May peace prevail on the Earth.
Gandhi is the father of nations.
He speaks at the press conference.

May peace prevail on the Earth!
Tenzin Kalden, 10 years old

From: Leonardo da Vinci "Gesichtsstudien"
(facial studies)

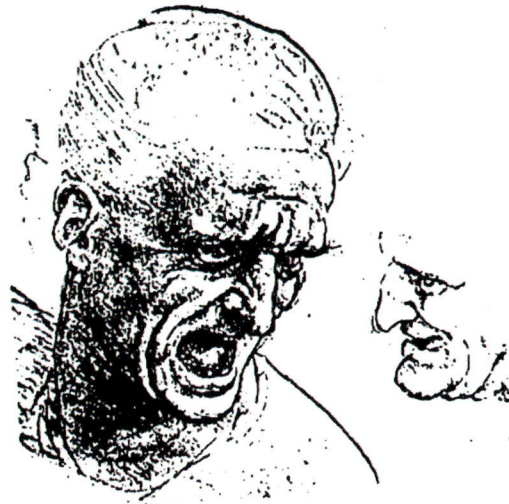

MAY PEACE PREVIAL ON THE EARTH

THE GHANDHISI THE FATHER OF NATIONS
HE CAN SPEACH to He PRESS Conference

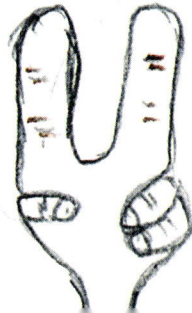

PEACE

His name is Mahatma Gandhi…
…and his real name was Mohas das Karamchanj Gandhi. He was born on 2nd October 1869 in Porbander in the state of Gujant (India). Later he was called "Mahatma" or "great soul".
After the independence of the people he became the father of the nation.
The Indians also call him "Babu".
His mother was a "Pious" lady.

Tenzin Wangmo, 13 years old, a girl, TCV Ladakh
Original: Tibetan and English

180

His name is Mahatma Gandhi
Tenzin Wangmo, 13 years old

From: Leonardo da Vinci "Gesichts studien"
(facial studies)

Name: Tenzin Wangmo.

Class - VI

School - Ani Gompa (Nangyal School)

age - 13

address - Swayambhu.

nationality - Tibetan)

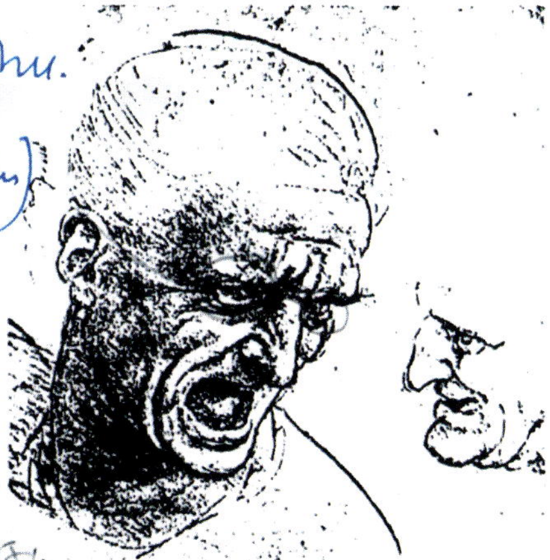

བོད་ཡིག་... (Tibetan script handwriting)

... (MAHATMA) ...

10 3

... (Babu) ...

HIS NAME IS MAHATMA GANDI AND HIS REAL
NAME WAS MOHAS DAS KARAMCHAND GANDHI. HE WAS
BORN ON OCTOBER 2nd 1869 AT PORBANDER IN THE STATE
OF GUJANT (INDIA) LATER HE WAS CALLED 'MAHATMA'
OR GREAT SOUL.

AFTER INDEPENDENCE THE PEOPLE OF
THE FATHER OF THE NATION. INDIAN ALSO CALLED HIM
BABU. HIS MOTHER WAS A PIOUS LADY.

181

Thoughts about the political situation in Tibet
In his picture Rigzin Dorje depicts the crossed flags of Tibet and India as a symbol of friendship between the countries - Tibet and India - and refers to the long-standing support of the Indian government concerning the Tibetan refugee policy.

Flags
This is a symbol of the world map.
These two flags are the Tibetan and the Indian flags.

Rigzin Dorje, 9 years old, a boy, TCV Ladakh
Original: English

Flags
Rigzin Dorje, 9 years old

From: Valery Bugrov, a sketch from "Heaven and Earth"

Choedak Sangpo presents a concrete situation in his picture, in which a Tibetan is violently attacked by a Chinese, then he gives more reasons to the reader why the Tibetans had to leave their country.

The Tibetans were not happy in Tibet…
…because the Chinese put force to the Tibetans, they also killed the Tibetans and destroyed monasteries.

Choedak Sangpo, 9 years old, a boy, TCV Ladakh
Original: English

184

The Tibetans were no longer happy in Tibet…
Choedak Sangpo, 9 years old

From: Leonardo da Vinci "Gesichtsstudien"
(facial studies)

Tibetan was not happy in Tibet beacoo Chines the Tibetan and bytocer to the Tibetan also Kill dostorny monestery

185

In his story Tenchoe uses strong vivid symbolism: *the caught fish* (in his picture: *the glittering fish in a net*) is compared to Tibet as an occupied country. The man who caught the fish represents the Chinese and Tenchoe dramatically explains as he sees it how they treat *this fish in a net*.

A man is catching a fish
For example the fish is in the net.
The fish looks like our country and the man looks like a Chinese.
The Chinese suppressed our country and killed our people, put them in prison. They also destroyed our monasteries and took our treasure to China.

186

Tenchoe, 13 years old, a boy, TCV Dharamsala
Original: English

A man is catching a fish
Tenchoe, 13 years old

From: a piece of red glittering paper

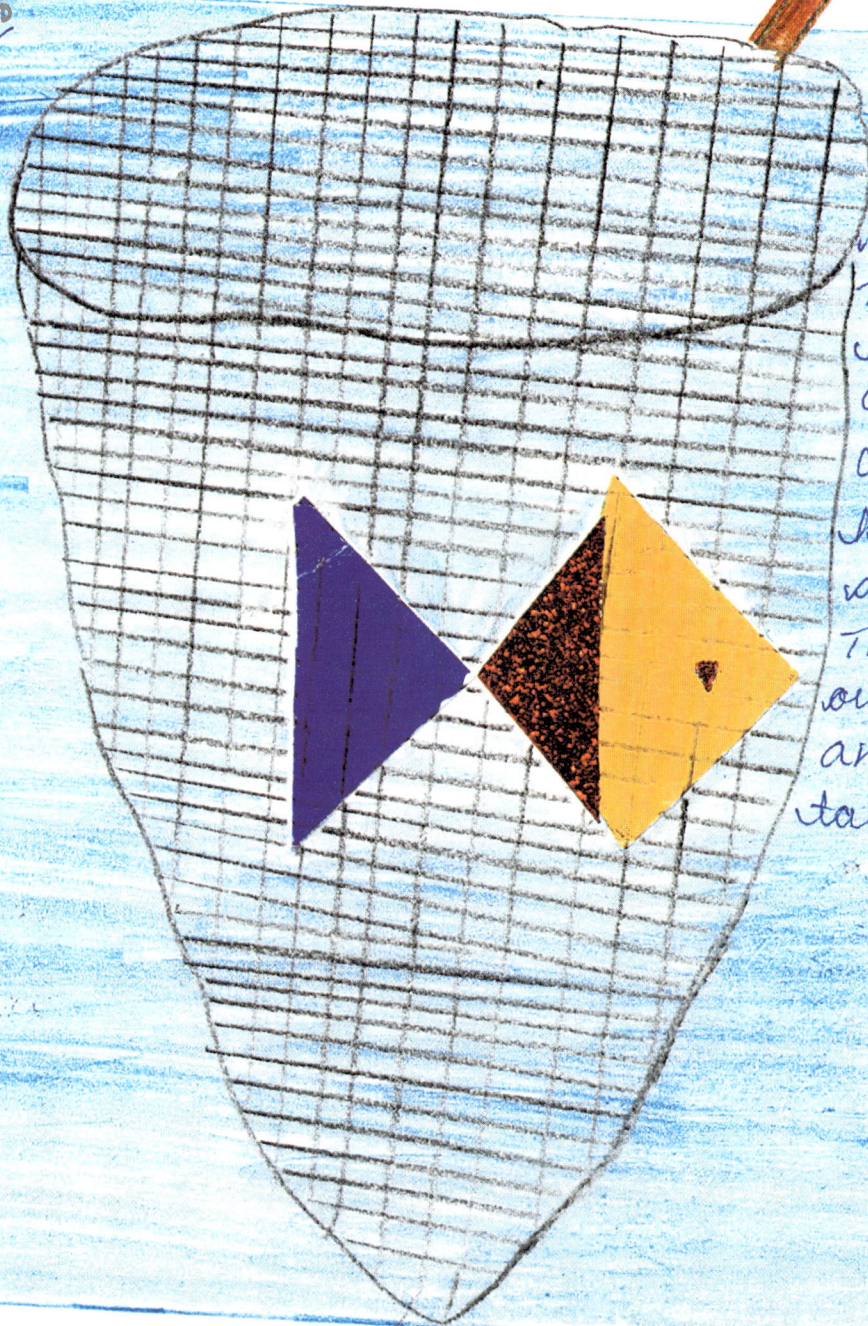

A man is catching a fish. A fish is in the net, look life our country and a man is look like Chines, Chines oppressed our country and killed our people and put in person. They also destroy our monastries and our treature take in China.

187

Tsering Wongdue's story *Snow land* (an emotional synonym for occupied Tibet) is also probably symbolic, he writes: *Birds come to the Snow land to help and bring peace to the Snow land Tibet*[57].

Snow land
The Chinese are giving troubles to the people of the Snow land Tibet. Birds come to the Snow land to help and bring peace to the Snow land Tibet.

Tsering Wongdue, 13 years old, a boy, TCV Dharamsala
Original: English

188

[57] This is an allusion to the famous poem of the 6th Dalai Lama:

Oh, white crane,
Lend me your wings
I am not far away from Lithang
And then I will return.

Snow land
Tsering Wongdue, 13 years old

Name Tsering Wongdue

age 13

address T.C.V school Dharamsala

nationality - Tibetan

boy

Snow, Land.

The chines are giving trobles to the people
of snow Land Tibet and the birds are come to
snow Land to help for become peace on the snow
Land Tibet

189

General thoughts about politics
All people in the world want peace with these words Ngawang Migmar appeals to the necessity of practical implementation of the topic *Peace*.

All people in the world like peace
But they don't know how to live in peace.
I think that if we don't harm each other is how to live in peace.

Ngawang Migmar, 11 years old, a boy, TCV Dharamsala
Original: English

All people in the world like peace
Ngawang Migmar, 11 years old

Name: Ngawang Migmar
age: 13
address: ~~Uppper~~ Uper T.C.V
nationality: Tibetan

ill the people in world like to peace but there don't know How to live in peace. I thought that ~~we~~ If wee cant ~~be~~ harm each other is how to live in peace.

Dawa Tsering and Tenzin Dolma eloquently express thoughts about two important socio-political aspects.

To give a speech on this occasion…
…is important for the improving society or its democratic government, or the social welfare of the society.
It is very important to know who has the opportunity to deliver it.

Dawa Tsering, 10 years old, a boy, TCV Ladakh
Original: English

To give a speech on this occasion…
Dawa Tsering, 10 years old

From: Leonardo da Vinci "Gesichtsstudien" (facial studies)

Giveing speech on the occassion is only for the improving society or their Democreating government or their social welfar living in the society so it is very important to deliver who has to opportunity to deliver it

Tenzin Dolma similar to Tsering Wongdue refers to the symbol of a bird:
A man without education is like a bird without wings...

A man without education is like a bird without wings
Nowadays education is the only and the best way to success. In the 21ˢᵗ century life is full of challenges.
And we have to take challenges. So, a man without education is like a bird without wings.

Tenzin Dolma, 12 years old, a girl, TCV Ladakh
Original: English

194

A man without education is like a bird without wings
Tenzin Dolma, 12 years old

From: artist's group *Die Schlumper* from the series "Treppensteiger" (stair climbers)

Educated
person

Uneducated person

195

Work

Sonam Yangzom describes the reasons for her professional wish: she would like to be a *doctor* in order to improve the situation of the Tibetans in Tibet. She explains the origin of this wish which is linked with her own biography.

I would like to be a doctor…

…because I want to help other people who are very ill. When I was small I wished to become a doctor. I saw that doctors are very nice and good because when I had big health problems, they nursed me and I was so happy. So I want to do like this.
I want to go to China and nurse all my Tibetan people.
I get a very good education for a doctor.

196

Sonam Yangzom, 13 years old, a girl.
TCV Dharamsala
Original: English

I would like to be a doctor…
Sonam Yangzom, 13 years old

Profession
I would like
to be a __Doctor__

Dr. Sonam Yangzom hosipital

Why? Please, explain!
I would like to bee a doctor. because
I want to help other people and very
illness man. When I was small I
wish to become a doctor and I see
doctor are very nice and good because I
have big sore and they nursed me
and I am so happy. So I want to
do like this. I want to wont to ching

and nursed my all
ibetan people. I have
become very good
education no doctor.

Tenzin Tsedup devotes his story to the profession of a *cook*. In his picture he presents some details of practicing this profession (for example, gas cooker, a sharp knife which he holds in the hand, etc.)

He is a cook
He makes food.
He cuts potatoes and apples with the help of his knife.
This is his main aim.
He makes food in the kitchen.

Tenzin Tsedup, 10 years old, a boy, TCV Ladakh
Original: English

He is a cook
Tenzin Tsedup, 10 years old

He is cook. He make foods. He cut the potata and Apple are cut with the help of knife. This is his main aim. He make the food in kitchen.

LOBSANG

Lobsang Tseden describes a harmonious working situation in an office. His story reflects his great inner contentment (*his face is full of joy*).

He is working in his office…
…and looking to the door side
He is sitting on his chair and he is looking so happy.
He is full of joy on his face.

Lobsang Tseden, 8 years old, a boy, TCV Ladakh
Original: English

200

He is working in his office…
Lobsang Tseden, 8 years old

From: Paul Klee "Schellenengel"
(Angel with the bell)

TSEDEN

201

He is working in his office and he is looking to the doorside He is sitting on his chair and he is looking so happy and he is full of joy on his face

Tsering Yankyi using the English pun "*do or die*" raises the topic *poverty* and *heavy work* in a developing country, and Psultrim also describes a typical scene from the rural working life of her surroundings in the Nepalese exile.

His choice is "do or die"[58]
He is the one who takes on all the heavy load.
I mean to say that he could solve his problems with his abilities and hard work.

Tsering Yankyi, 8 years old, a girl, TCV Ladakh
Original: English

His choice is "do or die"
Tsering Yankyi, 8 years old

From: artist's group *Die Schlumper* "Sisyphus"

[58] A pun in English: *do or die*

His choice is "DO OR DIE"

He is one who take all neave wud out I
mean to say that he would +solve his
problem though his ability and hard work

Once upon a time there was a man
His name was John.
He worked as a farmer.
He always went to the field for
farming.
He sold his crop in the market to earn
money for his family expenses.
This was his way of life.

Psultrim, 10 years old, a girl,
Katmandu, Nepal
Original: Tibetan and English

204

Name = Psultrim
age = 10
nationality = Tibetan.
School = Ani Gompa (Swaymabhu)
boy
girl ✓

Once upon a time there was a man
Psultrim, 10 years old

From: artist's group *Die Schlumper*
from the series "Treppensteiger" (stair climbers)

Free time

A palette of subjects is offered here: a visit to a party (which is not allowed), practicing bodybuilding as a kind of sport, as well as playing football which is practiced by many Tibetan boys with great passion.

11-year-old Thinley describes a boy who often goes to parties. This rather unusual topic is rather "disreputable": *he came back home on a ladder,* this means that at night he must creep secretly into his house?!

Party

There was a boy who went from one party to another.
He came back home on a ladder.

206

Thinley, 11 years old, a boy, TCV Ladakh
Original: English

Party
Thinley, 10 years old

From: artist's group *Die Schlumper*
from the series "Treppensteiger" (stair climbers)

There was a one boy. He was going to party.
after party he come back in home on ladder

Tenzin Dawa's topic *Bodybuilding* is also rather rare. Tenzin Dawa refers creatively to handlebars using Pablo Picasso's sculpture "bull's head".

Bodybuilding
This is the only muscles exercise.
For today and forever.

Tenzin Dawa, 10 years old, a boy, TCV Ladakh
Original: English

208

Bodybuilding
Tenzin Dawa, 10 years old

From: Pablo Picasso "Stierkopf" (bull's head)

THIS IS THE ONLY MUSCLE EXERCISE FOR TODAY AND FOR EVER

In the conclusion of this chapter there are four stories about football which is the most popular kind of sport at present besides cricket:

Tashi Gyurmey gives a hint at the worldwide enthusiasm about football. So today it is possible to watch international football matches on TV.

In the whole world there are children who play football
Here is the match between Triral and Songb.
Triral won the match.
The best player in Triral is Gyurmey.
He is the best player in the world.

210

Tashi Gyurmey, 9 years old, a boy, TCV Ladakh
Original: Tibetan

In the whole world there are
children who play football
Tashi Gyurmey, 9 years old

GYURMEY

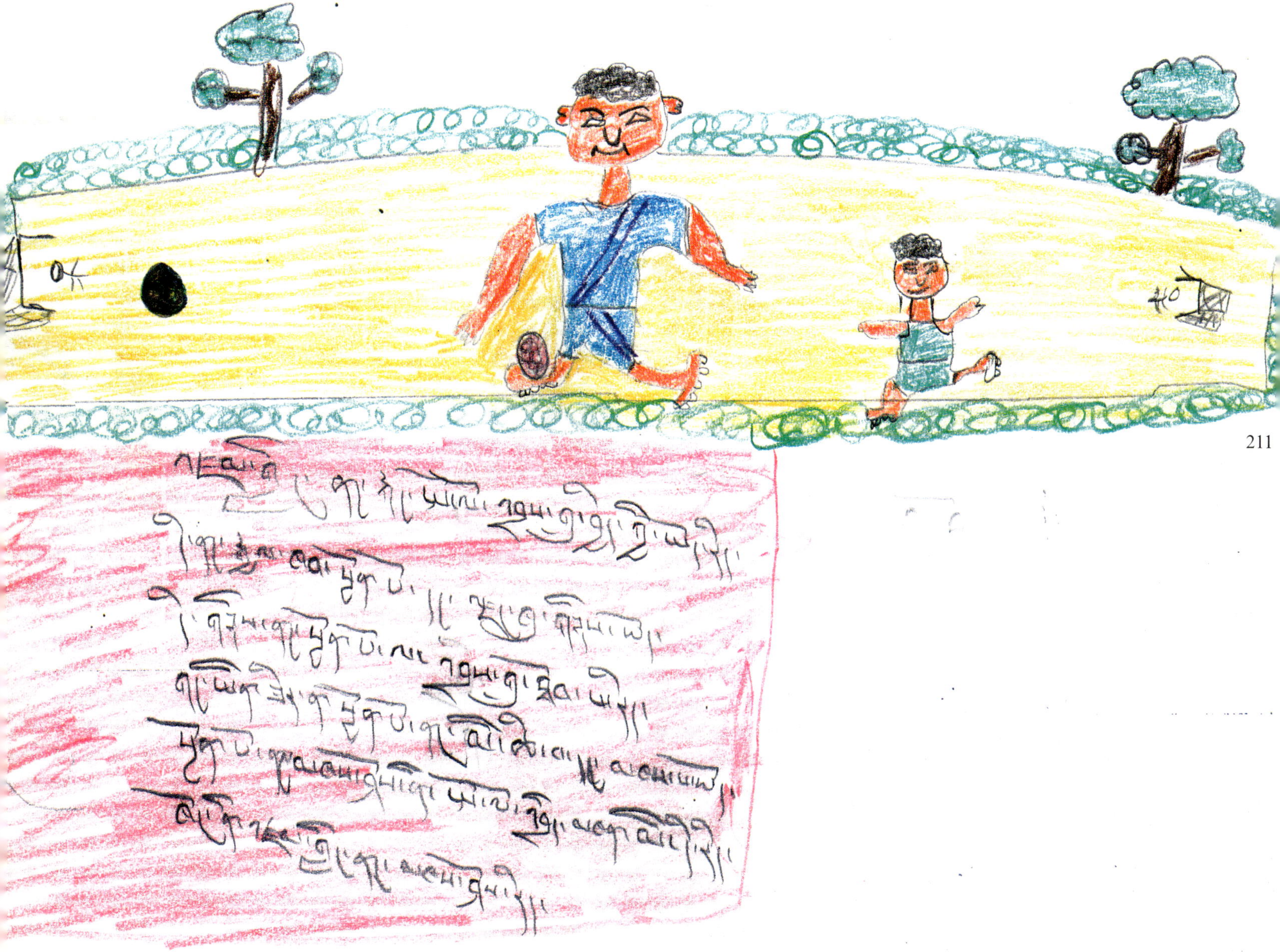

Jigmey Dolma (by the way a girl!) and Jigmey Uigen describe active and passive ways of taking part in football and Gonpo Dorje finally speaks about one man who plays football in the realm of dreams. Like in many previous examples in this book, both Jigmey Dolma and Gonpo Dorje end of their stories with an I-form that explains their great interest and self-identification with the described content.

He is tancing the ball and going to play football
The children are big.
His eye is as big as a football.
Tenzin is a football player.
I like Ladakh.

212

Jigmey Dolma, 8 years old, a girl, TCV Ladakh
Original: Tibetan

He is tancing the ball and going to play football
Jigmey Dolma, 8 years old

From: artist's group *Die Schlumper* "Sisyphus"

བཤགས་དང་རྗེས་ཡི་རང་བཀྲི་ཀུ་ཡི།། ཆོས་འཁོར་རྒྱ་ཆེ་བསྐུལ་བའི་ལུ་གུ།
ཞལ་ཡིཆུ་ག་བཞི་ཡི་ག་ཡི།། ཀུ་ཡ་བྱི་ག་ག་ཡ་བ་འཁྱུར་ལ་ཁྲོ་ཡ།
ཟ་ཚག་ག་ཡི།། བཤགས་དང་ཀ་ནི་ཉུ་ལ་ག་ཡ་ལ་ཁྲི་ག་ཡི།།
ར་ཀ་ར་ཀ་ལ་ལྡེ།། ཁ་ཚ་རྐུ་ཀུ་ལ་ཁྱེ་ར།།

One Sunday…
… there was a football match on the playground.
So he is watching the match and how they are
playing.
He also wants to play football.

Jigmey Uigen, 10 years old, a boy, TCV Ladakh
Original: English

One Sunday…
Jigmey Uigen, 10 years old

From: artist's group *Die Schlumper* from the
series "Treppensteiger" (stair climbers)

He dreams that he is playing football
Once there was a man.
He sleeps in our bedroom.
He dreams:
"I am playing football.
I am the one that kicks a ball
- that is a goal!"

Gonpo Dorje, 9 years old, a boy,
TCV Ladakh
Original: English

He dreams that he is playing football
Gonpo Dorje, 9 years old

From: artist's group *Die Schlumper* from the
series "Treppensteiger" (stair climbers)

one there are man. He sleping
in our beat room. He hadrema I
am to playing a foot ball.
I am one kicke a ball
I That is Goald.

NECHUNG ORACLE: the World Flower

Thanks to my friend Tsering from Mongolia who has been living in Dharamsala for many years, it was possible for me to meet Ven. Thupten Ngodub (the Medium of the State Oracle of His Holiness the Dalai Lama) in Nechung monastery and talk about my project. He promised me despite of his tight schedule to paint a picture for the project and, therefore, for the Tibetan children. Towards the end of my stay in Dharamsala in 2001 he presented his wonderful picture to me:

It is a fine drawing, done with crayons, in which one can recognize the world sphere. The globe in general appears as a blooming flower on a stem (that is why it is called *The world flower*). In the segments of the globe one can see the elements that make up our nature: air, water, wind and fire(up-down-left-right).

The world of our animals and plants in their natural surroundings (from the bottom upwards): the world of water with various kinds of fish, mammals in different landscapes like mountains and jungles, a man (from birth until death), finally birds and butterflies in the air.

His drawing in general is characterized by the deep symbolic knowledge of Tibetan Buddhism.

6.6. *We live in our Mother Earth's stomach…*
POEMS

Writing poems and practical use of poetry is historically recorded as the "didactic" means within the religious teachings and the tradition of high Tibetan Lamas.

Thus, for example, Milarepa (1040-1123), a great ascetic and one of the founders of Kagyuepa-school, became famous for his mystical songs.

The 6th Dalai Lama (Lama Tsangjang Gyatso, 1683-1706) is until now considered as a talented poet, especially his romantic love songs are very famous.

Like in a circle this book is concluded by poems. They have been written by children and teenagers of the TCV Dharamsala.

An overall view of the poems:
- to the drawing *The World Flower* by Nechung Oracle
  - to Valery Bugrov's *Heaven and Earth*
  - invocation of *Green Tara*

The World Flower
Painted by Nechung Oracle exclusively for the project in March 2001

218

MICRO- AND MACRO-COSMOS

The idea of one universal micro- and macro-cosmos seems to me especially worth emphasizing in this context, as it corresponds to the general idea of the drawing.

The concept that the basis for the entire cosmos, which are manifested on the large (macro) as well as on the small (micro), on the physical as well as on the psychological levels, has its systematic expression also in Tibetan Buddhism.

The thoughts rooted in the micro- and macro-cosmos system represent the perfection in multi-layered symbols; the cosmos is just the same as the spirit of Buddha. The idea of the identity of macro- and micro-cosmos is based on the belief that there are the equivalents and the connection between the micro- and macro-cosmos, between the material and the spiritual.[59]

The present oracle, Ven. Thupten Ngodup was born in Tibet in 1958 and is a descendent of the famous Tantric Master, Ngadak Nyang-relwa (1136 - 1204).

Following the Chinese invasion, he fled with his parents into exile to India and later joined the Nechung Monastry as a novice monk in 1971.

In 1987, he was recognized as the true successor of the previous Nechung Medium, who passed away in 1984.

He was officially enthroned in 1988 as the Nechung Medium, the Chief State Oracle of Tibet

Meeting with Nechung Oracle (Dharamsala)

219

[59]Cf. timphu.bhutan.at:81

The Phenomenon of oracles remains an Important part of the Tibetan way of life. The purpose of the oracles is not just to foretell the future. They are called upon as protectors and sometimes used as healers. However, their primary function is to protect the the Buddha Dharma and its practioners. In the Tibetan tradition the word oracle Is used for a spirit which enters those men and women who act as mediums between the natural and spiritual realms. The mediums are, therefore, known as *Kuten*, which literally means "the physical basis".

The oracle is the medium through whom Dorje Drakden (Nechung), the principal protector of the Dalai Lama and the Tibetan government, communicates with His Holiness the Dalai Lama and the kashag (cabinet). Major decisions of the state are also made in consultation with the Nechung Oracle. It is because of this that Nechung Kuten is given the rank of a deputy minister in the exiled Tibetan government hierarchy.

220

Dorje Drak-den (Nechung),
the principle protector
of His Holiness, the Dalai Lama
and the Tibetan government

"On formal occasions, the Kuten is dressed in an elaborate costume consisting of several layers of clothing topped by a highly ornate robe of golden silk brocade, which is covered with ancient designs…
On his chest he wears a circular mirror which is surrounded by clusters of turquoise and amethyst, its polished steel flashing with the Sanskrit mantra corresponding to Dorje Drakden.
…Altogether, this outfit weighs more then seventy pounds and the medium, when not in trance, can hardly walk with it."

Nechung Monastry, Dharamsala (Gangchen Kyishong)

Nechung monastry has an important place in the history of Tibet. It is the seat of Nechung, Tibet's State Oracle.

Nechung Oracle under trance

221

The world in which we live is a shining flower…
Poems to the picture by Nechung Oracle

The following three examples are the poems written by Tenzin Tsokyi, Ngawang Migmar and Jamyang Bokto. They were written in March 2002.

Praise on our mother Earth
From the deep of the ocean to the high blue sky
I see many, many living beings, all so bright and clean.
Some human beings have black, grey, yellow, and blond hair.
But all are the same because all are born from their mother's stomach.
All animals are busy talking with each other in their own language
and at the same time looking after their little ones.
All are happy and live in peace. The birds are busy searching for
long worms, and butterflies are busy sucking nectar from the flowers,
and the great bee is busy searching for a place to make a hive for her
little ones.
That's how our days and nights go on our beautiful mother Earth.

222

Tenzin Tsokyi, 13 years old, a girl, TCV Dharamsala
Original: English

To make the world the best place to live
In this world there are conflicts.
Pains, sorrows and wars.
When there is a birth, there is an end.
The end means death.
Sufferings of birth, getting sick and old, death.
But there are so many phenomena.
The art of silence and peace.
Look at the great beauty of nature.
The birds are singing in the sky.
The universe and everything…
Now we depend much on the plants
If we don't care for our plants,
One day it will be too late.
So all living beings should be blessed
To make the world the best place to live.

Ngawang Migmar, 13 years old, a boy, TCV Dharamsala
Original: English

Peom~

From ~~the~~ bottom my heart to the sky so blue,

I imazing that we the puppet made by God,

The world is shining flower we live,

The place we born and die,

The world is our mother,
We all the living thing are her sons,
The animals are our brother
The birds are our sister,

So, we ~~don't~~ are the one,

Who save our mother from die,

So, why we are killing each other

Why can't we unity again,

Name ~ Jang Bokto
Age ~ 14
School ~ Upper T.C.U. Dharamsala,

A poem
From the bottom of my heart to the blue sky I imagine that all creatures are made by God.
The world in which we live is a shining flower, the place we are born and die. The world is our mother. We, all living beings, are her sons, The animals are our brothers, The birds are our sisters.
So, we are the ones who save our mother from dying.
So, why we are killing each other; why can't we unite again.

Jamyang Bokto, 14 years old,
a boy, TCV Dharamsala
Original: English

223

A poem
Jamyang Bokto, 14 years old

We live in our Mother Earth's stomach
Mother Earth gives us clothes.
Mother Earth gives us food.
Mother Earth gives us home.
Mother Earth is like our mother.
Thank you, my dear Mother Earth.

Tenzin Tsokij, 12 years old, a girl,
TCV Dharamsala
Original: English

224

We live in our mother Earth's stomach
Tenzin Tsokij, 12 years old

From: Valery Bugrov, "Heaven and
Earth"(sketch)

Name: Tenzin Tsokyi
age: 12
address: T.C.V upper.
nationality: Tibetan.

We live in our mother ▮ earth. We
are in our mother earth's ▮ stomach
Mother earth give us cloths. Mother earth
give us food. Mother earth give us house.
Mother earth is like our mother.
Thak you my dear mother earth.

Green Tara

Oh, Tara, oh, green Tara,
You are my goddess.
I'm your follower,
Like a teacher and his student.

You are the one who shows the right way,
And saves me from going wrong,
You are the one whom I always believe,
believe in you forever.

Oh, Tara, green Tara,
don't ever leave me alone,
without you, far away,
like a bird without wings.

Jamyang Bokto, 15 years old, a boy,
TCV Dharamsala
Original: English

Poem: Green Tara
Jamyang Bokto, 15 years old

Green Tara

Oh, tara, oh green tara,

You are my god,

I'm your follower,

Like a teacher and,

his student.

You are the who show right pathe,

And save me from going wrong,

You are the one which I ever

~~think~~ believe,

Believeing you for future ever,

Oh, tara, green tara,

don't ever live me alone,

Without you, far away,

like a bird, without a wings,

Name~ Jamyang Bokto

Date - 27th March 2003.

Invocation of Green Tara

Tara represents is the embodiment of the protective activity of the inspired compassion. As the inspiration develops on the grounds of sympathy, Tara is called "Mother of all Buddhas of the three times".

Green Tara

Green Tara is a goddess. We, Tibetans, firmly believe in her.
She is a Buddhist goddess.
As for me, before going to bed and after getting up in the morning
I always pray to Green Tara and to all Buddhist gods to thank them for what I am now.
I go once every month to the temple to worship to the gods.
As for my emotions, when I am scared or in trouble
I see Green Tara in my mind and I start to pray for her help and when I'm happy I pray to Green Tara
and to all Buddhist gods to make me feel the feelings of happiness.

Tenzin Tsangyang, 14 years old, a girl, TCV Dharamsala
Original: English

Green Tara, Thangka from Buryatia (probably the 19th century), property of the author

LITERATURE

Bernstorff, Dagmar Grafin/von Welck, Hubertus (Hrsg.). 2002. *Tibet im Exil*. Baden-Baden

Brauen, Martin und Kantowsky, Detlef, Hrsg. 1982. *Junge Tibeter in der Schweiz*. In : *Konkrete Fremde*. Interkulturell vergleichende Studien der Arbeitsgruppe Entwicklungslander an der Universitat Konstanz (Schriftenreihe). Diessenhofen, Schweiz : Rueffer

Dalai Lama XIV (27.5.99) in einer Privataudienz zum Projekt *Tibetische Kinder im Exil*

Dalai Lama XIV; Howard C. Cutler. The Art of Happiness. Philadelphia, PA, USA: Coronet Books.

Dalai Lama XIV. 1990, 1998. Freedom in Exile. London, UK: Harper Collins Publishers.

Dalai Lama XIV. 1990, 1998. Freedom in Exile, p. 235

Diehm, Isabelle. 1997. *Migrantenkinder in der Grundschule*. Die Grundschulzeitschrift 106: 43-47.

Fischer, Gottfried und Riedesser, Peter. 1998. *Lehrbuch der Psychotraumatologie* (S. 288-292). Munchen, Basel: Reinhardt.

Grieder, Peter. 1990. *Tibet Land zwischen Himmel und Erde*. Olten: Walter.

Hausmann, Gottfried, 1935. Zur Aktualgenese raumlicher Gestalten. In: Friedrich Sander, Hrsg., *Ganzheit und Gestalt. Psychologische Untersuchungen* (S.289-333). Jena

Hausmann, Gottfried, 1965. Ganzheit und Aktualgenese in ihrer Bedeutung fur die Methodik des Unterrichts. In: Artur Kern, Hrsg., *Die Idee der Ganzheit in Philosophie, Padagogik und Didaktik* (S.135-156). Freiburg/Breisgau: Herder

Hilton, Isabel *Die Suche nach dem Panchen Lama*, Munchen: Beck 2002

International Campaign for Tibet. Tibetan Centre for Human Rights and Democracy Europe. *Das Bildungswesen in Tibet*. 2003. www.tchrd.org

International Campaign for Tibet. Deutschland e.V. Gefahrliche Flucht Bedingungen tibetischer Fluchtlinge. Deutschland. 2003.

International Work Group for Indigenous Affairs (IWGIA). The Indegenous World 2001-2002.

Krumm, Hans-Jurgen. 2001. Kinder und ihre Sprachen lebendige Mehrsprachigkeit. Wien : Eviva.

Krumm, Hans-Jurgen. 2002. Mein Bauch ist italienisch... Kinder sprechen uber Sprachen. In: Grundschule Sprachen 7/2002., S. 37-40.

Lavizzari-Raeuber, Alexandra. 1989. Thangkas. Rollbilder aus dem Himalaya. Kunst und mystische Bedeutung. Koln: DuMont.

Mattausch, Jutta. 1996. *Ladakh und Zanskar* (S. 266-269). Bielefeld: Reise Know-How.

Meyer, Franz. 1961. *Marc Chagall Leben und Werk* (S.380). Schauberg Koln: M.Du Mont.

Ott-Marti, Anna-Elisabeth. 1980. *Probleme der Integration von Tibetern in der Schweiz*. Ruemlang/Zurich, Schweiz: Robert Hofmann.

Pema Jetsun. 1996 *Tibetan's Children's Village (Information Brochure)*. Dharamsala, India: Archana.

Pema, Jetsun. 1997. *Zeit der Drachen: Die Autobiographie der Schwester des Dalai Lama*. Hamburg: Hoffmann und Campe.

Pema, Jetsun. 2002. *Tibetische Kinderdorfer*. In: Bernstorff, Dagmar Grafin/von Welck, Hubertus (Hrsg.). 2002. *Tibet im Exil*. Baden-Baden

Rabkin, Gabriele.1995. *Der Engel fliegt zu einem Kind. Anregungen zum freien Schreiben und Gestalten aus der bildenden Kunst*. Stuttgart: Klett.

Rabkin, Gabriele. 1996. *Ways to Writing and Culture Especially for Children and Youth from Socially Underprivileged Background*. International Workshop Hamburg, UNESCO Institute for Education, 29 31.1.1996. Hamburg

Rabkin, Gabriele u.a., Hrsg. 1998. *Fantasien von Kindern aus aller Welt*. Stuttgart: Klett.

Rabkin, Gabriele. 1998. *Schreibanregungen in Theorie und Praxis*. Hamburg: LIT.

Rabkin, Gabriele. 2000. *Die schone Hexe. Anregungen zum freien Schreiben und Gestalten aus der Ganzheits- und Gestaltpsychologie*. Stuttgart. Klett.

Rabkin, Gabriele. 2001. *Kindern das Wort geben. Ein interkulturell-kreativer Arbeitsansatz, aufgezeigt an der Arbeit mit tibetischen Migrantenkindern*. In: International Review of Education, S.97-121. Niederlande: Kluewer.

Santideva. 1981. *Eintritt in das Leben zur Erleuchtung* (S.60, Kap. 5, Vers 94). Munchen: Diederichs.

The Archive of the Jewish Museum, Ed. o.J. *Children?s Paintings from the Ghetto Terezin*. Prague.
Tibetan's Children Villages.o.J. *The Clever Rabbit, a Tibetan Folktale*.

Tsepak, Rigzin. *Modernitat und Uberlieferung: Das tibetische Schulwesen*. In: Bernstorff, Dagmar Grafin/von Welck, Hubertus (Hrsg.). 2002. *Tibet im Exil*. Baden-Baden.

Yeshi, Kim. Losel. O.J. *Alternative Forms of Tibetan Art. Dharamsala*. India: Counsil for Religious and Cultural Affairs of His Holiness the Dalai Lama.

The Government of Tibet in Exile. 12/1999. *Tibetan Exile at a Glance*. www.tibet.com/exilglance.html.

www.onlinekunst.de/januar/20_01_Hikmet_Nazim.htm

www.rolfklein.de/Buratien.html

www.tibet-institut.ch/institut.html

www.beyars.com/kunstlexikon/lexikon_8370.html

www.timphubbhuthan.at:81

www.tibet.de/tib/stupabau.html

www.nechungnyc.org

www.tibet.com/Buddhism/nechung_hh.html

230

Fotos: Gabriele Rabkin, exept:
p.48   Valery Bugrov
p.2,7   Yoshi Fredisdorf
p.22   Sonam Wangchuk
p. 62/63, 69   unknown
Cover (front) Hayo Heye, Hamburg, Germany
Cover (end)   Maxim Rabkin

ACKNOWLEDGEMENTS

Firstly, I would like to express my sincere gratitude to His Holiness the Dalai Lama for His inspiration and support for this project. My thanks also go to all children, colleagues, dear Friends and helpers who supported and gave their Advice to this project.

Special thanks to:

In India, Dharamsala
Jetsun Pema, Director TCV Headoffice
Rinchen Khandro Choegyal, former Minister of Education, Director of the Tibetans Nuns Project
Tsewang Yeshi, Co-Director TCV Headoffice
Nechung Oracle
The Office of His Holiness - especially Tenzin Thakla and Ven. Lhakdor
Phuntsok Tsering, Headmaster, Upper TCV Elementary School and his colleagues and pupils
Bhiksuni Tenzin Yeshe and Bhiksuni Tenzin Dao (Australia/Dharamsala)
Tsering (Mongolia/Dharamsala)
Tashi Gyatso, Guesthouse Pemathang

Delhi
Dr. Dagmar Grafin Bernstorff
Surojit Banerjee (Allied Publishers)

Leh, Ladakh
Collegues and pupils of the TCV Ladakh (Choklamsar)
Yoshi Fredisdorf (USA)

In Kathmandu, Nepal
Walter Ahlhorn (Kathmandu/Hamburg)
Maylis Chevalier (Kathmandu/Hamburg)
Sonam Wangchuk

In Russia
Ulan-Ude, Burjatia
Lama Oleg and his pupils (Ivolginsk Monastry)

Kaliningrad
Igor Isajev
Dmitry Demidenko

Moscow
Ngawang Gelek, Representatives of His Holiness in Moscow
Tatjana Metaxa (Museum of Eastern and Fareastern Arts)

St.Petersburg
Andrey Trentjew

In Rikon, Switzerland
Roswitha Reinhard (Tibet Institute)
Peter Grieder (Tibet Institute)

In Hamburg, Germany
Dr. Paul Belanger (former director of UNESCO-Institute for Education (Canada)
Lia Hamburger and „Gustav Prietsch-Stiftung"
Ven. Maria Viktoria, Tibetan Center
Marianne Masson
Phurbu, Restaurant "Tibet" and Palden
Helmut Steckel (Tibetan Initiative)

I would especially like to thank "Karla und Alfred W. Adickes-Stiftung" for their support and Dr. Christopher McIntosh for checking the translation.

My thanks are due as well to my family:
Maxim Rabkin, my son and
Dr. Peter Pieler, my father, for patient support with PC and co-reading
Valery Bugrov for his advice as an Artist and big support of publishing.

Furthermore I thank all those not mentioned here, who supported us with their advice and practical help.

In this book there was room for only some pictures and stories chosen out of a big collection.
I would like to thank all the Tibetan children in many parts in the world who gave me their contributions and could not be represented in this book.